The Way of the Mystics

WALKING WITH GOD:
THE SERMON SERIES OF HOWARD THURMAN

1. *Moral Struggle and the Prophets*
2. *The Way of the Mystics*

THE WAY OF THE MYSTICS

Howard Thurman

Edited by
Peter Eisenstadt and Walter Earl Fluker

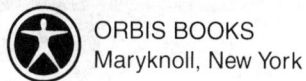
ORBIS BOOKS
Maryknoll, New York

ORBIS BOOKS
Maryknoll, New York 10545

Founded in 1970, Orbis Books endeavors to publish works that enlighten the mind, nourish the spirit, and challenge the conscience. The publishing arm of the Maryknoll Fathers and Brothers, Orbis seeks to explore the global dimensions of the Christian faith and mission, to invite dialogue with diverse cultures and religious traditions, and to serve the cause of reconciliation and peace. The books published reflect the views of their authors and do not represent the official position of the Maryknoll Society. To learn more about Maryknoll and Orbis Books, please visit our website at www.orbisbooks.com

Texts by Howard Thurman copyright © 2021 by Anton H. Wong for the Thurman Family.
Introduction and commentary copyright © 2021 by Peter Eisenstadt and Walter Earl Fluker
Published by Orbis Books, Box 302, Maryknoll, NY 10545-0302.
All rights reserved.
No part of this publication may be reproduced or transmitted in any form or by any means, electronic or mechanical, including photocopying, recording, or any information storage or retrieval system, without prior permission in writing from the publisher. Queries regarding rights and permissions should be addressed to: Orbis Books, P.O. Box 302, Maryknoll, NY 10545-0302.
Manufactured in the United States of America

Library of Congress Cataloging-in-Publication Data

Names: Thurman, Howard, 1899-1981, author. | Eisenstadt, Peter R., 1954- editor. | Fluker, Walter E., 1951- editor.
Title: The way of the mystics / Peter Eisenstadt and Walter Earl Fluker, editors.
Other titles: Sermons. Selections
Description: Maryknoll, NY : Orbis Books, 2021. | Series: Walking with God ; volume 2 | Includes bibliographical references and index. | Summary: "Sermons by Howard Thurman on mystics and mysticism."—Provided by publisher.
Identifiers: LCCN 2021005395 (print) | LCCN 2021005396 (ebook) | ISBN 9781626984387 (trade paperback) | ISBN 9781608339013 (ebook)
Subjects: LCSH: Mysticism—Sermons.
Classification: LCC BV5082.3 .T48 2021 (print) | LCC BV5082.3 (ebook) | DDC 248.2/2—dc23
LC record available at https://lccn.loc.gov/2021005395
LC ebook record available at https://lccn.loc.gov/2021005396

Contents

Acknowledgments and Editorial Note — vii

Abbreviations — ix

Howard Thurman: A Brief Chronology — xi

Introduction — xiii

Men Who Have Walked with God: The Mystics
Introduction
12 April 1953, Fellowship Church — 1

William Blake
10 July 1950, Fellowship Church — 10

Lao-Tse
19 April 1953, Fellowship Church — 19

Buddha
3 May 1953, Fellowship Church — 25

Plotinus
10 May 1953, Fellowship Church — 34

Saint Augustine
24 May 1953, Fellowship Church — 43

Mahatma Gandhi
7 June 1953, Fellowship Church — 54

Saint Francis
14 June 1953, Fellowship Church — 62

Jane Steger
21 June 1953, Fellowship Church   72

Meister Eckhart
5 July 1953, Fellowship Church   82

Jacob Boehme
12 July 1953, Fellowship Church   91

Thomas à Kempis
17 July 1953, Fellowship Church   103

Additional Sermons and Lectures

The Religion of the Inner Life
ca. 1950, Fellowship Church, San Francisco   112

Mysticism and Social Change: God as Presence
12 July 1978, Pacific School of Religion   121

Mysticism and Social Change: Rufus Jones
25 July 1978, Pacific School of Religion   141

Selected Bibliography   161

Index of Names   165

Acknowledgments and Editorial Note

The editors thank Hazel Monae Johnson, Nora Graciela De Arco, and Dr. Silvia P. Glick for their assistance, and Robert Ellsberg of Orbis Books for his support of this project. A special thanks is extended to Anton Wong and Suzanne Chiarenza, grandchildren and trustees of the Howard Thurman Estate, for their permission to pursue this publication. Finally, the editors would like to acknowledge their gratitude to Dr. Edwin David Aponte and the Louisville Institute for making possible research time from 2016–2017 for Walter Earl Fluker through the Louisville Foundation Sabbatical Grant.

Most of the texts in this volume are taken from transcriptions of audiotapes; the transcriptions were made under the auspices of the Howard Thurman Education Trust in the 1970s. When possible, we have checked the accuracy of the transcriptions against the original audio tapes. The editors have tried to retain the informal, improvisatory quality of the sermons, while eliminating double starts, some interjections and tangents, and have silently corrected obvious mistakes, mispunctuation, and resolvable confusions in the transcriptions. The original audio sources differ in their comprehensiveness; some include initial meditations and opening illustrative quotations; others do not. Whenever possible, the editors have included the full sermon or lecture. Thurman used gendered language to refer to persons or people in general throughout his career, and the editors have not altered his language. The editorial procedures used in preparing this volume closely follow the editorial statement in Walter Earl Fluker, ed., *The Papers of Howard Washington Thurman: The Wider Ministry, Vol. 5* (Columbia: University of South Carolina Press, 2019), lvii–lxi.

Abbreviations

HT   Howard Thurman

HTC   Howard Thurman Collection, Howard Gotlieb Archival Center, Boston University

PHWT   Walter Earl Fluker, ed., *The Papers of Howard Washington Thurman,* volumes 1–5 (Columbia: University of South Carolina Press, 2009–19).

WHAH   Howard Thurman, *With Head and Heart: The Autobiography of Howard Thurman* (New York: Harcourt Brace Jovanovich, 1979).

Howard Thurman:
A Brief Chronology

1899	Born in Florida on 19 November, raised in Daytona
1915–1919	Attends Florida Baptist Academy/Florida Normal and Industrial School in Jacksonville/St. Augustine
1919–1923	Attends Morehouse College, Atlanta, Georgia
1923–1926	Attends Rochester Theological Seminary (Rochester, NY)
1926	Marries Katie Kelley; Minister of Mount Zion Baptist Church, Oberlin, OH
1927	Daughter Olive is born
1928	Professor of religion, Morehouse and Spelman Colleges
1930	Katie Kelley dies
1932	Marries Sue Bailey; campus minister and professor of religion, Howard University
1935–1936	Chair of Negro Delegation on "Pilgrimage of Friendship" to South Asia
1944	Becomes co-pastor of Fellowship Church in San Francisco, pioneering interracial church
1949	Publishes *Jesus and the Disinherited*
1953	Becomes dean of chapel and professor of spiritual resources and disciplines at Boston University
1963	Travels to Africa, teaches at Ibadan University in Nigeria
1965	Retires from Boston University, returns to San Francisco, directs activity of Howard Thurman Education Trust
1971	Publishes *The Search for Common Ground*
1979	Publishes *With Head and Heart: The Autobiography of Howard Thurman*
1981	Dies on April 10

Introduction

> Mysticism is one of the truest forms of human thought. It is religion in its most concrete and exclusive form. It is finding a way to God. I say finding *a* way to God and not *the* way to God. . . . [The mystic] reduce[s] all of the multiple and conflicting elements of reality to one continuous whole. In his moment of illumination, the mystic realizes this unity. It is in this experience that he is principally convinced that the *real* experience is one of unity rather than disunity. ("The Mystic Way," ca. 1938)
>
> The mystic rests his case upon the primary contactual[1] experience of God. It is first hand. He considers himself as standing within the experience itself. ("Mysticism and Social Change," February 1939)
>
> [Mysticism is] the response of the individual to a personal encounter with God within his own soul. Such a response is total, affecting the inner quality of the life and its outward manifestations. ("Mysticism and Social Change," 1959)

If there is one point of agreement in discussions of Howard Thurman's distinctive understanding of religion, during his lifetime and subsequently, it is that he was a mystic. As early as 1932, Thurman was being described in the Black press as "the Negro mystic," or reporting on "Reverend Thurman in one of his characteristic mystical attitudes."[2] In 1942 the

---

1. Of or relating to contact.
2. Richard H. Bowling, "The Guide Post," *New Journal and Guide* [Norfolk, VA]; Lucius L. Jones Jr., "A Version of the Thurman-Bailey Nuptials," *Atlanta Daily World*, 15 June 1932.

Pittsburgh Courier hailed Thurman as "one of America's great mystics."[3] Similar encomia continued throughout his life for this "mystic, scholar, poet and author," or "clergyman, educator, [and] mystic."[4] The secondary literature on Thurman has volumes titled "the mystic as prophet," or on his "philosophical mysticism."[5] There are substantial accounts about Thurman in books such as *American Mysticism: From William James to Zen*.[6]

Howard Thurman was a mystic, but unlike many mystics he spoke very little about his own mystical experiences and was far more comfortable speaking and writing about mysticism in general, or, as in this volume, exploring his personal canon of great mystics. He encouraged spiritual exploration, without the expectation that those in his hearing would become mystics. He was always conscious of the likelihood that his discussions of mysticism would be misunderstood. He opened his first published writing on mysticism, from 1934, with the following disclaimer: "Perhaps there is no word in our language that has been as completely misunderstood and as freely interpreted by unintelligent sincerity as 'mysticism.'" As he noted, everyone from Harry Houdini to Mahatma Gandhi had been labeled as a mystic.[7] Despite his best efforts, he knew that many saw mysticism pejoratively, as something airy and abstruse, impractical and metaphysical. Lester Granger, the executive secretary of the National Urban League in 1941, offered the barbed compliment that while Thurman's talks "frequently smack of mysticism . . . every now and then he throws his mysticism away and delivers his audience a real sock on

---

3. Peter Dana, "Dr. Thurman Speaks on Indian Question," *Pittsburgh Courier*, 29 August 1942.

4. "Elect Howard Thurman to American Academy," *Chicago Defender*, 13 June 1959; J. Y. Smith, "Howard Thurman, Clergyman, Educator, Mystic Dies," *Washington Post*, 16 April 1981.

5. Luther E. Smith *Howard Thurman: The Mystic as Prophet* (Lanham, MD: University Press of America, 1981); Anthony Sean Neal, *Howard Thurman's Philosophical Mysticism: Love against Fragmentation* (Lanham, MD: Lexington, 2019).

6. Hal Bridges, *American Mysticism: From William James to Zen* (New York: Harper & Row, 1970), 51–60.

7. HT, "Review of Mary Anita Ewer, *A Survey of Mystical Symbolism*," *Journal of Religion* 14 (October 1934): 383–84. Ewer's book would long be one of Thurman's favorite texts on mysticism.

its intellectual solar plexus."[8] Thurman's writings attempt to rescue mysticism from this sort of condescension and derision. He frequently used the title "Mysticism and Social Change" or some near variant to demonstrate that what seemed oxymoronic to scoffers like Granger was nothing of the sort. There was a mysticism that sought to change the world rather than retreat from it.[9]

Thurman was a mystic long before he acquired an adequate vocabulary to describe it. He once told an interviewer that "when I was born God must have put a live coal in my heart, for I was his man and there was no escape."[10] But his religion was personal and unconventional, seeking God out of church, out of doors, in a world with ghosts, angels, and pervaded by the divine presence.[11] It began at the moment of his birth, when he was born with a caul, with the amniotic sac covering his face, behind the veil, a rare occurrence that his mother and grandmother thought conveyed the gift of second sight, of clairvoyance. However, they believed second sight was a supremely unlucky gift, bringing only misfortune to its possessors; and so, to ward it off, they pierced his ears. But it didn't entirely work. "How deeply I was influenced by this 'superstition' I do not know," he wrote in his autobiography, adding that he had always believed that he had, in some measure, retained the ability of "second sight."[12] There were other childhood "superstitions." He sought in nature, out of doors, out of

---

8. Lester Granger to Virgil Louder, 23 December 1941, in Folder 6, Box 28, HTC.

9. For Thurman's writings on socially involved mysticism, see "Mysticism and Social Change," in PHWT 2: 190–222 (February 1939); "Mysticism and Social Change" (public lecture, Berkeley, CA, 1959), in Folder 5, Box 8, HTC; "Mysticism and Social Action," in *Lawrence Lectures on Religion and Society* (Berkeley, CA: First Unitarian Church of Berkeley, 1978); "Mysticism and Social Change" (fifteen lectures, Pacific School of Religion, July 1978), in Folders 37–38, Box 8, HTC; "Mysticism and Social Action," *AME Zion Quarterly Review* 92, no. 2 (October 1980): 2–13.

10. Jean Burden, "Meditation on Howard Thurman on the Occasion of His Memorial Service April 10, 1981," in Howard Thurman Paper Project Files, Boston University.

11. HT, "Mysticism and Social Change," Lecture 5: [God as Presence] (12 July 1978), printed in the current volume. See also HT, "Religious Commitment" (ca. 1978), in Folder 25, Box 4, HTC; HT, "The Binding Commitment," in Folder 24, Box 4, HTC.

12. WHAH 263; See also Mircea Eliade, *Shamanism: Archaic Techniques of Ecstasy* (Bollingen Series 76; Princeton, NJ: Princeton University Press, 1964), 16; and

church, a unity that he could not find among humans. As he wrote in *The Search for Common Ground*, from his earliest years "a tendency—even more, an inner demand—for 'whole-making,' a feel for a completion in and of things, for inclusive consummation."[13] The lessons of his elders, especially those his grandmother, Nancy Ambrose, imparted to him a haunted and enchanted world, of threats and rewards, of hidden linkages between apparently unconnected events. Hers was a syncretistic Afro-Christian worldview, though he nowhere discusses the likely sources of his grandmother's spirit lore.

Thurman looked for other explanations for his spiritual inclinations. He became, like his grandmother and mother, a dutiful churchgoer, and he flourished in the world of Black Baptists; but a gap remained between his Christian beliefs and his out-of-doors mysticism. Of his time as an undergraduate at Morehouse College (1919–1923), one of his instructors, his lifelong friend Benjamin Mays, would write, "I believe that he showed signs then of possessing more mysticism in his religion than the average person, so much so that I am inclined to think that he was considered queer by some of the students and professors."[14] During his three years at Rochester Theological Seminary (RTS; 1923–1926) he was taught little or nothing about mysticism from his instructors. However, he did learn from RTS that "all dogma, all theology—however wonderful they may be—are always a little out of date, because they are rationalizations—using that word in the best sense of the word—they are rationalizations of religious experience," not the dynamic, fluid experience of the divine that was part of his own personal life.[15]

Thurman's understanding of his own mysticism was greatly deepened by two encounters in the 1920s. In 1925 he discovered the work of the South African novelist, pacifist, and feminist, Olive Schreiner (1855–1920). Schreiner was a bold religious thinker, largely post-Christian. "I did not identify as being mystical," Thurman said in 1978; despite

---

Clarence E. Hardy III, "Imagine a World: Howard Thurman, Spiritual Perception, and American Calvinism," *Journal of Religion* 81, no. 1 (January 2001): 78–97.

13. HT, *The Search for Common Ground* (New York: Harper & Row, 1971), 76.

14. Benjamin E. Mays to Mary Jenness, 12 February 1936, in PWHT 1: 323–25.

15. Roberta Byrd Barr, "A Creative Encounter: Interview with Howard Thurman, Part 1 (14–15 February 1969)," in Folder 30, Box 16, HTC.

"certain experiences which were a part of my life since I was a little boy until I began studying the life and the works of Olive Schreiner."[16] Like Thurman, Schreiner was at her core a nature mystic, and after reading her, he would write, "it became possible for me to move from primary experience, to conceptualizing that experience, to a vision inclusive of all of life."[17] The second encounter, both personal and intellectual, was the semester he spent in 1929 with the American scholar of mysticism, Rufus Jones at Haverford College. From Jones he learned the vocabulary and the history of mysticism that would guide his thinking for the remainder of his life. This is discussed at greater length in Thurman's lecture, printed in the current volume, on his study with Jones.[18]

After his semester with Jones, Thurman began to preach about mysticism and taught courses on mysticism at Howard University and was increasingly identified as a mystic by journalists and others. Thurman's first substantial published discussion of mysticism was four lectures he delivered in 1939 at Eden Seminary near St. Louis on the topic of "Mysticism and Social Change."[19] (Although they were printed in the seminary bulletin, they were not widely circulated, and Thurman himself either never knew, or forgot, about their publication until their rediscovery in the 1970s.) Thurman would write about mysticism in numerous sermons, lectures, and meditations, and he made mysticism the subject of three books, *The Creative Encounter* (1953), *Mysticism and the Experience of Love* (1961)—first delivered as the Rufus Jones Memorial Lecture—and *Disciplines of the Spirit* (1962.)[20]

This book prints some of Thurman's most significant unpublished sermons on mysticism. At its centerpiece are two sermon series he gave at Fellowship Church in 1950, and again in 1953, with the same title and many of the same overlapping subjects, "Men Who Have Walked

---

16. HT, "Mysticism and Social Change: Lecture 1," (5 July 1978).

17. HT, ed., *A Track to the Water's Edge: The Olive Schreiner Reader* (New York: Harper & Row, 1973), xxviii.

18. HT, "Mysticism and Social Change: Lecture 12: [Rufus Jones]" (25 July 1987), printed in the current volume.

19. HT, "Mysticism and Social Change," in PHWT 2: 190–222.

20. *The Creative Encounter: An Interpretation of Religion and Social Witness* (New York: Harper & Brothers, 1954); *Mysticism and the Experience of Love* (Wallingford, PA: Pendle Hill, 1961); *Disciplines of the Spirit* (New York: Harper & Row, 1962).

with God." These were sermons on some of his favorite mystics, on his personal canon of the mystical tradition. (The subjects were largely, but not entirely male.) They range chronologically from the Buddha to Thurman's twentieth-century contemporaries. From the two sermon series the editors are publishing thirteen sermons. This is supplemented by several other writings on mysticism: a 1950 sermon "The Religion of the Inner Life," and two lectures from a course he taught in 1978 at the Pacific School of Religion on "Mysticism and Social Change."

Thurman recognized a wide variety of different types of mysticism but patterned his broader explanations of mysticism on his own experiences. In 1939 he wrote that he did not claim "to have scaled the heights of rarefied illumination so vivid to the mystic in his moments of clarity, but I have lived for a long time in the stream of the mystic's experience."[21] Thurman, drawing from Rufus Jones and other students of mysticism such as Mary Anita Ewer and Evelyn Underhill, came to see mysticism as a distinct kind and category of religion, and that all mystics, in their experience of God, shared something profoundly alike, transcending their outward creedal affiliations.[22]

Because he probably thought words superfluous and did not want his vision of mysticism to occlude anyone else's path, he rarely described his own mystical experiences in any detail, preferring to help others "center down" and find their own paths of God. One exception is this poetic account of a hilltop epiphany from 1939. As often was the case with Thurman, a response to nature inspired his deepest spiritual impulses:

> I journeyed to a hill top at close of day
> Darkness stole upon the valley beneath as sleep on a tired brow
> Silence pursued me all the day
> Won at last—
> Exhausted I lay at his feet . . . [ellipsis in original]
> No sense of senses, time—space all
> Awareness of self spread out till I and all
> Around me run together

---

21. HT, "Mysticism and Social Change," in PHWT 2: 191.
22. For Underhill, see HT, "Mysticism and Social Change: Lecture 14," 27 July 1978.

In one expansive, streaming, liquid quiet.
Suddenly with a start—time began
The heavy cares of the years seemed lighter now—
God so near
I was radiant
With holy light. [23]

In a 1959 lecture, Thurman described four types of mysticism. There were mystics who "stand in a relationship of personal response to a God they conceive in more or less personal terms," common in Catholic, Protestant, and Hindu mysticism. This included mystics whose experience of God focused on Jesus, labeled by Thurman as "Christ mystics."[24] There were mystics who respond to "an infinite more or less intellectually conceived, and the attitude of response defined in one of contemplation." In this group he placed mystic traditions such as Daoism, Neo-Platonism, and the Kabala. The third group were practitioners of the "mysticism of the Light Within." Thurman characterized these mystics "as having a trustful attitude towards inner experience. It is their insight that they touch a divinely formed point of contact with God within the Soul." The fourth category was the "mysticism of occult science," various methods of obtaining psychic insight into matters otherwise hidden.[25] Although Thurman had a surprisingly avid interest in occultism, in precognition, synchronicity, in faith healers, and in seers such as Edgar Cayce—an interest he largely kept out of his talks on mysticism—he was preeminently a mystic of the Light Within.[26]

Thurman's mysticism of the Light Within was patterned on the practices of the Quakers, something he was first exposed to when he studied with Rufus Jones. Jones also introduced him to the mystic that Thurman

---

23. HT, "Mysticism and Social Change," in PHWT 2: 201–2.
24. See the lecture on St. Augustine, printed in the current volume.
25. HT, "Mysticism and Social Change" (1959), Folder 5, Box 8, HTC.
26. For Thurman's interest in Rosicrucianism, see Thurman to Rev. J. E. Dunn, 11 March 1937, in Folder 16, Box 24, HTC. For his interest in Edgar Cayce, see Walter N. Panhke to Thurman, in PHWT 4: 193–97. For his meeting with faith-healer Harrie Vernette Rhodes, see "Mysticism: Lecture 6" (April 1973), in Folder 37, Box 8, HTC; and Marguerite Harmon Bro, *In the One Spirit: The Autobiography of Harrie Vernette Rhodes, as Told to Marguerite Vernette Rhodes* (New York: Harper & Brothers, 1951).

always thought best exemplified this tradition, the thirteenth-century German Dominican priest Meister Eckhart, who taught that "there is an 'uncreated element' in the soul of man that is the God within," and much of Thurman's mysticism was developing and explaining spiritual techniques to find this inner God, such as silences, detachment, and meditation, which he discussed in his book *Disciplines of the Spirit* and elsewhere. Eckhart's influence on Thurman is discussed at greater length in the sermon on Eckhart printed in the current volume. A consequence of Thurman's emphasis on the Light Within meant that for him "the mystic experiences unity" with God, he wrote in 1939, but "not identity," a unity with God that enhances, rather than dissolves, the mystic's personality and presence.[27]

This was a mysticism active in the world. To use a distinction of Rufus Jones that Thurman made his own, it was a mysticism of affirmation rather than negation, which he understood as "working out in a social frame of reference the realism of their mystic experience."[28] Thurman gave numerous lectures on the subject of mysticism and social change or social action. But he always made clear that mysticism and social change were distinct, though ultimately inseparable. Douglas Steere, who first met Thurman at the time of his study with Rufus Jones at Haverford College, later a prominent Quaker theologian and writer on mysticism, wrote in a tribute to Thurman in 1975 that Eckhart's lesson that "you can only spend in good works what you have earned in contemplation" must have lodged deeply in "Howard's mind and spirit for it has been a theme song of his ever since."[29] He opened his 1939 lecture series "Mysticism and Social Change" stating that because "it has been necessary for me to participate both passively and actively in what is known as the social struggle," his was a mysticism that had practical, political consequences.[30] The mystic is "under obligation to achieve the good which in some profound sense is given in the moment of vision."[31] In affirmation mysticism, for

---

27. HT, "Mysticism and Social Change," in PHWT 2: 208.
28. HT, "Mysticism and Social Change," in PHWT 2: 213.
29. Douglas V. Steere, "Don't Forget Those Leather Gloves," in *Essays in Honor of Howard Thurman on the Occasion of His Seventy-Fifth Birthday, November 18, 1975* (ed. Samuel Lucius Gandy; Washington, DC: Hoffman, 1976), iii.
30. HT, "Mysticism and Social Change," in PHWT 2: 191.
31. HT, "Mysticism and Social Change," in PHWT 2: 214.

Thurman, "the distinction between personal and social religion" becomes "artificial and unrealistic."[32] The affirmation mystic's vision of the good is connected to the social struggle, not primarily "because of any particular political or social theory" or because of "humanitarianism or humanism." Rather, the mystic is "interested in social action because society as he knows it ensnares the human spirit in a maze of particulars so that the One cannot be sensed nor the good realized."[33] Rufus Jones was one of two mystics profiled in "Men Who Have Walked with God" that Thurman had actually met. The other was the model for socially involved mysticism, Mahatma Gandhi.

If Thurman's was a mysticism of the Light Within, it was also a mysticism of the boundlessness and connectedness of nature and human community. In 1944, probably for the first time, he offered what would become a signature aphorism, a mystic tautology, the "utterly astounding fact" that "life is alive." Life, Thurman further explained, is "even more alive than any particular manifestation of life." Life pervaded everything, even apparently inert objects like rocks and stones. If this was an insight of Olive Schreiner, it was something he knew intuitively before he read her work. In 1978 he told the journalist and historian Lerone Bennett Jr. that "ever since I can remember I have felt that there is no binding or absolute separation between the segment of life that is Howard Thurman and life."[34] Indeed, he speculated, it might be possible to get beyond "the wall, barrier, or context" that separates one form of life, one species, from another, perhaps by means that were currently unacknowledged by contemporary science.[35] What this meant for Thurman was, as he wrote in 1944, if "the cosmos is the kind of order that sustains and supports life and its potentials," then it "sustains and supports the demands that the relationships between men and between man and God be one of harmony, integration, wholeness, all that we mean by love." If "life is alive," then life

---

32. HT, "Mysticism and Social Change," in PHWT 2: 214

33. HT, "Mysticism and Social Change," in PHWT 2: 216.

34. Lerone Bennett Jr., "Howard Thurman: 20th Century Holy Man," *Ebony* 33, no. 4 (February 1978): 85

35. HT, *The Search for Common Ground*, 67.

is indivisible. Segregation and artificial separation between people and peoples equaled death.[36] This was Thurman's deepest mystical vision.

There is a story Howard Thurman liked to tell about Reinhold Niebuhr (1892–1971), the distinguished American theologian. During the 1930s and early 1940s the two men were quite close, and Niebuhr was a frequent guest preacher at Howard University, where Thurman was dean of chapel. On one occasion, they talked into the wee hours, having a "typical no-holds-barred discussion about religion and our society and the rest of it." When Niebuhr taught his next class at Union Theological Seminary he talked about his discussion. There was one Black student in the class. After the class he came up to Niebuhr and said: "I'm glad you mentioned that man. He is the great betrayer of us all. When this Thurman fellow came up out of Florida and began to talk around, many of us who were much younger were sure that at last someone had come who would be our Moses. And what did he do? He turned mystic on us!" At this point in telling the story, Thurman would laugh heartily.[37] Thurman liked being the butt of his own stories, but for Thurman, mysticism, at its highest, unites one's public and private self in a shattering moment of transforming clarity.[38] Like Moses at the burning bush, finding his God, and finding his life's mission, to free his people from their bondage.

---

36. HT, "The Cosmic Guarantee in the Judeo-Christian Message" (June 1944), in Folder 11, Box 7, HTC; reworked as "Judgment and Hope in the Christian Message," published in 1948, and reprinted in PHWT 2: 242–47.

37. Albert J. Raboteau, "In Search of Common Ground: Howard Thurman and Religious Community," in *Meaning and Modernity: Religion, Polity, and Self* (ed. Richard Madsen et al.; Berkeley: University of California Press, 2002), 157. For another version of the anecdote, see HT, "Mysticism and Social Action," 26.

38. See extended discussion of the public and private spheres of Thurman's mystical thought in Walter Earl Fluker, "Leaders Who Have Shaped U.S. Religious Dialogue," in *Howard Thurman: Intercultural and Interreligious Leader,"* volume 2 of *Religious Leadership: A Reference Handbook* (ed. Sharon Henderson Callahan; Thousand Oaks, CA: Sage Publications, 2013), 571–78.

Men Who Have Walked with God: The Mystics

Introduction

12 April 1953
Fellowship Church

In "Men Who Have Walked with God" Thurman offered sermons on his personal canon of mystics and mystical traditions. The sermons ranged chronologically from the "Axial Age," which saw the birth of many of the world's great religions, to the early twentieth century, including two persons of his personal acquaintance, Rufus Jones and Mahatma Gandhi. (The editors are printing an alternative piece by Thurman on Jones.) The obscure spiritual writer Jane Steger is the only woman included.

Most of the sermons are on Christian topics, though there are several sermons on Eastern mysticism and one on the non-Christian Roman philosopher Plotinus. Thurman delivered two sermon series titled "Men Who Have Walked with God," at Fellowship Church, one in the summer and fall of 1950, and another longer series in the spring and summer of 1953, consisting of thirteen sermons.[1] Although the bulk of the sermons printed here are from the 1953 "Men Who Have Walked with God" series, the editors have omitted from it two sermons, those on the Brahman mystics and the

---

1. The 1953 "Men Who Have Walked with God" sermons are in Folder 4, Box 11, HTC. The extant sermons in the 1950 "Men Who Have Walked with God" series are on Jacob Boehme, William Blake, Rufus Jones, and Mahatma Gandhi, in Folders 50–58, Box 11, HTC. The editors are printing the sermon on Blake and the 1953 texts for Boehme, Jones, and Gandhi. A 1961 sermon series he gave at Marsh Chapel, "The Inward Journey," included sermons on Jacob Boehme, Plotinus, Meister Eckhart, St. Augustine, and St. Francis and are in Folders 18–21, Box 13, HTC.

Renaissance artist Fra Angelico.² They have included one sermon from the 1950 series, on William Blake.

In the sermons on individual figures, Thurman tries to convey something of their personalities and their personal belief systems. In several of the sermons in the series, on Plotinus, Meister Eckhart, Jacob Boehme, and others, Thurman, usually not concerned with the details of theological systems, seems almost to revel in the complicated details of the specific mystical systems he discusses, as if he is encouraging his listeners to create their own theologies (and in the case of William Blake, their own mythologies) as they explore their personal relation to God.

In this introductory sermon from April 1953, following the opening meditation, Thurman provides one of his most succinct explanations of his own understanding of mysticism. For Thurman, the mystic believes "that we are surrounded by an all-pervasive Spirit of God," which "Spirit is in me," and, in personal terms, can "make direct contact with that Spirit without going outside myself." However, to guard against mistaken belief, the mystic needs to develop spiritual disciplines to test and understand that moment of insight and retain enough flexibility to be ready for additional promptings of the Spirit.

Although Thurman, following Rufus Jones, makes a distinction between "affirmation" and "negation" mysticism, this is not central to his argument in this sermon or the "Men Who Have Walked with God" series.³ Thurman here argues against too simple a division between worldly and unworldly mysticism and that even the most seemingly unworldly mystics were sure that they were "in touch with terrible energy, terrible energy" and wanted to make their lives "a point of focus through which that energy hits its mark in the world then the redemptive process can work." And for Thurman, "that is why the way of the mystic is so difficult and yet in some ways so simple."

---

2. The two sermons were excluded for reasons of space limitation. Brahman mysticism is also discussed in the sermon on the Buddha.

3. For Thurman on "affirmation mysticism," see, for example, PHWT 2: 213.

Men Who Have Walked with God: The Mystics 3

In many-sided activities, there is so much that engages the mind, and ensnares the emotions, that again and again, we are wanderers, lost in the midst of our own private and collective wildernesses, with no sense of being at home anywhere, in anything, at any time. Our enthusiasms wax hot and cold. One day life is full, and the wave is high and the sun bright, and the hours pass quickly and we seem no longer frayed, and then the next day, the day is long, dreary, and we wonder how it felt to rise with freedom and abandon on the crest of the wave.

It is wonderful therefore to sit together, to be enveloped by a single moment, and feel the presence, and sense the lights and shadows of those who sit near us. It is good to be caught in the creative silence, surrounded by the brooding presence of God. And perchance, as we wait together in the quietness, some new light may be thrown upon old problems, some fresh hope may give wings to spirit to which despair is the familiar. Perhaps a sense of forgiveness for sins committed, for errors done, for blundering stupidities that have wrought havoc in other people's lives. All this may be the miracle for us, as we wait together in the quietness. O love of God, without which life has no meaning, and no harbor, leave us not alone with our little lives, our broken dreams, our insistent problems, but invade our spirit with thy vitality, that we may be renewed in all the ways of our lives, that we may turn from this place, this day, with all that is within us, washed and purified and refreshed. We seek this with simplicity of heart, and with quiet faith and confidence that thou would not deny thy love to thy children. O God our Father, Amen.

I shall begin this morning a series which bears the same title and will include before I'm finished some of the same minds and spirits about whom we talked some two years ago under the same title, the title of a book by [Sheldon] Cheney.[4] The title was not original with Cheney because it comes out of the Old Testament. I would like to lay the ground-

---

4. Sheldon Cheney, *Men Who Have Walked with God: Being the Story of Mysticism through the Ages Told in the Biographies of Representatives Seers and Saints with Excerpts from Their Writings and Sayings* (New York: Alfred A. Knopf, 1945). Cheney's book contains ten short biographies of mystics. Seven of Cheney's subjects—Lao-Tse, the Buddha, Plotinus, Meister Eckhart, Fra Angelico, Jacob Boehme, and William Blake—were also treated by Thurman in his two "Men Who Have Walked with God" sermon series. Sheldon Cheney (1886–1980), a native of Berkeley, California, was a

work for our thinking together. It is just a little risky to discuss anything which has to do with mysticism in California. In some other parts of the United States, it is not as risky. Now that I have said it—and it isn't necessary for you to think it—we can go on now.

There are two or three basic insights upon which the mystic rests his total position, if indeed we may think of it in such formal terms. The first insight is that there is an all-pervasive Spirit, time-transcendent, space-transcendent, that gathers up into itself the total gamut of human experience. That's very important, because any persons who have thought much about mystical religion, which from my point of view, is genuine religion, tend to divide themselves into two groups. Those that say that mysticism is negative, that it is life-denying, that it pulls man away from the involvements of his life, that its watchword is detachment; and because it insists upon detachment, upon withdrawal, it is negative and because it is negative it is against life, and because it is against life there can be no morality in it! No morality! And if there is to be an ethic, if we are to be concerned with values or value judgments, then we must be moving out toward life; we must be in the stream of life.

Now, the basis for this observation is twofold. In the first place, a part of it is true. When you study the lives of these men and women who have explored the aspect of experience that opens up into the infinite, you see there are two aspects in experience. This side of experience that is measurable, we can put it into words that we can add up, that we can define. But there is another aspect to the same experience that opens in another direction, and when we look into that direction, we can't quite define it, we can't get meaning out of it. It's almost like looking at your watch. You look at your watch and you know what time it is, and as soon as you look at your watch and close it, then someone says, "What time is it?" and then you must look at your watch again! Now why? Because the first time you looked at your watch you looked at it for yourself. You looked at it in such a manner that did not have to be unscrambled, and as soon as someone made a demand upon you with reference to time, then you have to relocate this knowledge of which you were already sure but you had to relocate it in another context, moving out this way.

---

prolific author on the arts and the theater. *Men Who Have Walked with God* was one of Cheney's few books on a spiritual topic.

Now, all experience is like that! [In] the simplest relationship that means anything to you, you discover there are aspects to it that are quite measurable, that you can define. You love your child, you get up early in the morning, you get breakfast for the child, which in one sense are manifestations of this feeling-tone that you have; but curiously enough, now if someone said to you, "Now, pick out the one thing that you do for your child that *proves* that you love your child," you'd back away from that, because no one thing is quite able to do that, to contain all that the experience says, because the open end of the experience opens out into the infinite, you see. As long as you're looking this way, you can measure [it] out, as you do toothpaste out of one of these tubes, but looking from within another context, looking back at the source from which it comes, you aren't able to reduce it to a manageable unit, except to *experience* it! You know it! But you can't prove it! For the moment you begin trying to prove it, you say to yourself that means you aren't sure of it! For the things of which I am sure I don't have to prove! They are! But I can't escape the necessity for trying to prove it all the time. Now that is what the mystic is trying to say. One aspect of his interpretation of his experience moves out into time-space involvements, moves out into activities; but as he is observed it seems as if what he's really doing is withdrawing from all activities and finding his meaning and his significance in a dimension that has nothing to do with this world and with his time-space involvements. Let's take this overall background and break it down a little and see what we have.

I began by saying that the great and first basic principle of the mystic's interpretation of life is that we are surrounded by and enveloped by an all-pervading Spirit and that Spirit is the reality. And there are some who say that Spirit is the *only* reality and that everything else is shadowy seeming. (We may not think that.) Now the mystic takes another step. He is [part of] the creation, as all other life is, as all other things are, [part of] this all-enveloping Spirit. The human personality has deep within it that which is part and parcel of this all-inclusive, all-pervasive divine Spirit. To use the words of one about whom we shall be talking in some weeks, "the beyond that I seek is within."[5] That's what he's talking about. That I am not only created by this Spirit—this all-pervasive Spirit of God—but

---

5. The reference is to Meister Eckhart; see the sermon on him printed in this volume.

that within me is not a manifestation of the Spirit of God but *the Spirit of God*. And when, therefore, I seek within myself to commune with the Spirit of God, there is available to me, without any "go-betweener," primary, immediate, direct living contact with this living Spirit. Those are the two pillars about which the whole mystical insights rest, that we are surrounded by an all-pervasive Spirit of God, which Spirit is the Creator of life and the world, and which Spirit is in *me*. And that Spirit which is in me is the real thing, and I can make direct contact with that Spirit without going outside myself.

Now, that is why the mystic seems always to be at war with the institution. For the institution says that there is a formula that must be operative before you can experience this; certain ceremonials through which you must pass; the knee must bow in a certain way; you must be in a certain kind of place, built a certain way, with what is called an altar in front of it; or you must have some individual who himself has been set aside as the unique handler of the inner life or lives of men. He has to present you before this Spirit, that you must attach in your prayers a certain formula. Well, the mystic says, all right, for anybody who feels that that is what he has to do, but it doesn't mean anything to me because that's going all the way around Robin Hood's barn, as it were, to get into the door when the door is in me and *no man* can shut it! No man. That's why he's always a dangerous man! Suppose he's mistaken? Suppose he's mistaken?

You remember the story in [William] McCombs's "How I Made Woodrow Wilson President"? After McCombs had spent considerable time—according to the story which he wrote, he spent a fortune and lost his health practically in going all over the country and finally precipitated the landslide[6]—Woodrow Wilson was the next president, and they went to the summer home outside of Princeton to talk about who would be "what" and make these great decisions. When McCombs walked into Wilson's study, Wilson invited him to a chair and then he stood with his

---

6. In one of the few true three-way presidential elections in American history, Wilson, with 42 percent of the vote, defeated the Progressive Party and Republican candidates Theodore Roosevelt and William Howard Taft, who split the usual Republican vote, leading to a commanding Electoral College victory by Wilson, who won the electoral vote, respectively, 435 to 88 to 8.

back against the door and addressed McCombs as follows: "McCombs, I owe you nothing. God made me President!"[7] Now, when he's talking like that there isn't anybody who can say he's wrong! No! You can't say he's wrong! Who are you to say he's wrong? But suppose, but suppose he misread the signals? And there is released in him as a result of the conviction that arises in his spirit, inspired by that affirmation, a strength and a power and an endurance that nothing else in the world can give a man! And suppose he's mistaken? There is nothing more destructive in life than a man who is *sure*. Sure that he walked through the door that no man can shut and there the secret was given him! And on the basis of that secret he becomes as if he were ten thousand men! Nothing more deadly if the man didn't tarry long enough to get it straight. And who knows what tarrying long enough to get it straight is? Sometimes it takes thirty years to know whether or not a simple thing you did was an error! Sometimes it takes forty years! And indeed, a man may live his entire life profoundly convinced that his movements are in accordance with what seems to him to be the right ways of life, only to discover that he was mistaken! Therefore, that is why the mystic always goes back again and again and again and again, testing, testing, testing! He is unwilling to risk a single moment of transcendent ecstasy. That is a part of the meaning of the disciplines about which we will be talking these next Sunday mornings, disciplines that these various men found necessary. Very interestingly, not one of them, having spent hundreds of hours in the spiritual disciplines, as they are called, ever says that if the disciplines are followed, that which moves directly as the result of the disciplines, will be an active, dynamic awareness of the presence of God. No, the responsibility of the discipline is to keep the spirit pliable, to keep it from getting set, so that

---

7. William F. McCombs (1875–1921) was a native of Arkansas who attended Princeton University and Harvard Law School. He became active in Democratic politics and advised New Jersey governor Woodrow Wilson on his 1912 campaign; he was named chairman of the Democratic National Committee the same year. In his posthumous memoir of the 1912 campaign, he relates that after congratulating Wilson on his election, he was told, "Before we proceed, I wish it clearly understood that I owe you nothing . . . remember, that God *ordained I should be the next president of the United States*" (William F. McCombs, *Making Woodrow Wilson President* (ed. Louis Jay Lang; New York: Fairview Publishing, 1921), 2080.

when the Spirit of God moves, it won't do this, but it will move inside! And that is why however holy the mystic is, when you talk with him, one thing he's always sure about is that he is so far away from the living fruition of God in his life that the distance he is away is as the East is from the West!

Now, one more thing and then I'll stop. The all-pervading Spirit that creates all of life, including human beings, deep within the individual, says the mystic, there is God. That God is available. "Speak to him, for the spirit may meet, nearer than hands and feet"—there's that insistence.[8] And that the disciplines, because they keep the Spirit active, they keep the relatedness supple, and then there is the final thing: the necessity for relating the spiritual energy generated by this communion about which we shall be talking, these days, to relate that to the world of function. Even a mystic sect like the Essenes, who were very active during the time of Jesus, who withdrew from all participation, in the struggle of the Jewish community for freedom from Rome, who went into the hills, wouldn't cut their hair,[9] prayed. They were not withdrawing from the struggle, but they were sure that the only way that would destroy the empire was their way of working, They withdrew from cutting a Roman's neck off or doing a lot of other things out here, but they were not withdrawing from the struggle.[10] They felt that the way to do it is to move underneath the foundation that stabilizes the evil order; and if you move at that level, when you stir everything that's above you, you'll begin to crumble [it] and [it

---

8. "Speak to Him, thou, for He hears, and Spirit with Spirit can meet—/ Closer is He than breathing, and nearer than hands and feet" (Alfred Lord Tennyson, *The Higher Pantheism* [1869] ll. 11–12).

9. Thurman is probably confusing the Essenes with the Nazarites. In the Hebrew Bible, Nazarites vow to serve God, usually for a specific period of time, during which, among other restrictions, they must refrain from cutting their hair.

10. The Essenes were a contemplative and communal Jewish sect that flourished in Palestine during the Second Temple era. In 1937 Thurman had written that the Essenes were "life-negating" mystics who showed "no profound concern for the problems incident to the national life of the Jew ("The Significance of Jesus I: Jesus the Man of Insight," PHWT 2: 51). The 1947 discovery of the Dead Sea Scrolls, likely produced by the Essene community at Qumran [now in the West Bank], documents that often expressed fiercely national sentiments, probably changed Thurman's views. For Thurman on the Dead Sea Scrolls, see PHWT 4: 149n26.

will] fall because there is no power less than the power of God that is capable of withstanding the power of God. Therefore, if I can release, as a living channel, the living energy of God into the situation, anything that is less than that is in the situation that will be destroyed. Now that is what the mystic does with social action. He's no coward sticking his head in the sand, praying to God because he's scared or because he doesn't have nerve to do anything else; but he is sure that he is in touch with terrible energy, terrible energy, and if his life can be a point of focus through which that energy hits its mark in the world then the redemptive process can work, and that is why the way of the mystic is so difficult and yet in some ways so simple. And we shall see, during the next eight, nine, ten weeks what happens in the life of a man when this is his orientation, whether his religion is Buddhist, or Greek, Protestant, Catholic, or Jewish, or no religion.

WILLIAM BLAKE

10 July 1950
Fellowship Church

It is not surprising that Thurman was an admirer of the English poet, painter, engraver, and visionary mystic, William Blake (1757–1827).[1] In this complex sermon, in trying to explain Blake's esoteric theology and religious philosophy, Thurman states that Blake had "double vision," the ability to peer through the visible and see the invisible links between all things. As Thurman read Blake, they both shared a philosophy that saw the unity of all living things as representing a lost original unity.[2] When Blake looked at a person, he was able to see that each person is also "the roar of the lion; man is the song of the nightingale; man is the grass; man is the stone; man is the sand which is the gray hair of the earth." For Thurman, Blake's message was that "every time I sacrifice my ego" I get closer to the original unity." With selfless love, making sacrifices on behalf of "the sick birds or the dog with the broken leg, when I withhold my will to destroy the ant or the rat," I can begin to "come home and disrobe myself of self-consciousness and be the eternal as I was originally. Therefore, all of life becomes a process by which I overcome all the barriers that separate me from you" and come to recognize the unity of life.[3]

---

1. Original in "Men Who Have Walked with God: William Blake" (10 July 1950), in Folder 59, Box 11, HTC. William Blake (1757–1827) spent almost his entire life in London. He was apprenticed to an engraver and became a professional engraver and lithographer in 1782. He started to publish his books of poetry in the 1780s, almost all of them illustrated by Blake himself. Despite having a circle of admirers, his work was little appreciated during his lifetime, and he often faced financial hardships.

2. See, for instance, HT, "Judgment and Hope in the Christian Message," in PHWT 3: 242–48, and his various writings on community that culminated in HT, *The Search for Common Ground* (New York: Harper & Row, 1971).

3. For an earlier statement on Thurman on the evil of self-love, see "The Significance of Jesus III: Self-Love" (September 1937), in PHWT 2: 60–67.

We come this morning to the second [sermon] in part 2 of the series Men Who Have Walked with God. We are thinking together about just a tiny facet, perhaps, or segment of William Blake, the English poet and mystic and, perhaps, eccentric.

Last Sunday we talked about Jacob Boehme,[4] a man who profoundly influenced Blake because they were working away at the same basic aspect of experience and meaning and values. It is very disturbing and almost maddening in the quality of confusion to try to bring together in one swirling brace of minutes a meaningful picture of Blake and Blake's insight. But we shall work along and go as far as we can.

Of course, Blake was born, despite all of the emanations and illuminations; he was born, just as everybody else. He belongs to the end of the eighteenth century and the early part of the nineteenth century. He was one fortunate human being in having a wise parent who was sensitive to his needs and who did not try to fit him into a mold that [would] give him shape but destroy his spirit.[5] When his father saw that what he, the father, had in mind for Blake was no good for Blake based upon Blake's consistent reaction to what his father had in mind for him, the father then began taking his clues from what he observed about the life and the growing edges of his son. He served as an apprentice in lithographing and engraving; he learned that art very well during the first period of his life. And while he was in process of learning, his master assigned him to do sketches and drawings from certain of the objects in Westminster Abbey. For some eight or nine years he was a denizen of Westminster Abbey—a very fortunate young being.[6] He learned many things, felt many things. He was married finally. The first person with whom he was in love did not return his love, and he found somebody else. This somebody had pity on him, and he was moved by the quality of her compassion and was sure

---

4. For Boehme, see "Men Who Have Walked with God: Jacob Boehme" (12 July 1953), printed in the current volume.

5. James Blake, William's father, was a hosier, a maker of stockings and socks.

6. During Blake's apprenticeship, he was engaged to make a number of drawings of aspects of Westminster Abbey. The Abbey, built from the tenth through the thirteenth century, has been the site of every coronation of English and British monarchs since 1066. Its Gothic architecture influenced Blake's mature artistic style.

that that compassion which she provided for him was the thing that he would need all the rest of his life. He was afraid to act on that immediately, so he took a year to think it over, and at the end of the year he was more convinced that he had been at the beginning of the year, and they were married.[7] She was not a scholar. As a matter of fact, when they were married she could not read or write, but her love for Blake was so great and her understanding of him was so complete that almost without being tutored she reached into his mind and gathered to herself the things that would make her more useful to his needs. It is tremendous. When he would have his inspirations and he could not sleep because of the wild horses racing in his brain, he would get up and she would get up too, and she would sit sometimes all night holding his hand while these things were going on in his mind. She lived for Blake. It was an indulgence for her, and in the end it may not have helped him very much—I don't know, but that is off the point.

He did not get along with people too well because he had a mind of his own. He was always trying to see something and get at something and express something that other people didn't quite see and express, and he was forthright and direct and honest so one need not be surprised that his life was involved in a series of explosions of one kind or another.

He was a prolific writer and painter; his poetry is delicate and beautiful in its earlier stages, and it becomes more visionary and symbolic and mystical—it becomes a bit more difficult to follow. He died at the age of seventy in very limited circumstances but without a sense of having been deserted by life. It seems that he died a happy man. In the most superficial manner, that is the story of Blake's life as far as the chart is concerned.

Now what was this strange man trying to do? What was he after? What was the unique quality of his mysticism? Let us go to work on that for a little now.

You will recall that last Sunday we talked about the universe which Boehme had created. It is very important that we should begin at the same point with Blake. As a matter of fact, I sometimes think that it is important to begin at that point with any human being. How few of us take the time to try to think through what he really thinks about life and

---

7. After a failed relationship, Blake married Catherine Boucher (1762–1831).

its purpose. How many times do you let your mind wrestle with where you came from, how the world got started, what is life, what is the meaning of all of it, how can we account for this and this and this, how can we fix the multitudinous character of my experiences into some kind of creative synthesis that will give meaning to the central pulsing of my life so that in the living of my ways I will seem to myself to be involved in a process that is rational and moral: how often do you do that?

These men did that. Blake did it, and he had an interesting kind of universe. So don't sit in your seat now and smirk over the awkward, stupid, hair-brained thing that Blake talked about. Don't do that; just match it by what you think. If you don't think anything, well, we will go on.

We see in Blake in the first place a man who had always double vision, at least double vision. The inner, the outer. The outer was merely that through which he looked at the inner—he and Boehme were alike in that. All externalities, all manifestations, all of the things we see have at least no basic reality in themselves.

We look through these at the reality. The universe, if we constructed it very simply, would be this. There are what Blake called eternals.[8] They are not involved in time and space. We don't know where they are, you see, because the moment you raise the question of where, location, you are talking about time and space. These are outside of time and space, these eternals. Now one eternal decided that it would say, "I"—"I exist." These eternals are all separate, but they are all the same. They are many eternals but there is only one eternal. One of them decided that it would pull off from this unity, and say "I." The moment that happened, there was a rupture in the unity, you see, and a chain reaction set in motion. This eternal became eternity, and eternity has a time-space smack about it as over against [the other eternals].

---

8. The eternals, in Blake's dense personal mythology, are the named and unnamed members of the divine family, self-creating, outside of space and time. The chief eternals were the four Zoas: Tharmas (the bodily aspect of humanity), Urizen (human reason), Luvah (human emotions), and Urthona (human imagination). Guides to Blake's personal mythology include S. Foster Damon, *A Blake Dictionary: The Ideas and Symbols of William Blake* (2nd ed.; Lebanon, NH: Dartmouth University Press, 2013); and Leopold Damrosch, *Eternity's Sunrise: The Imaginative World of William Blake* (New Haven, CT: Yale University Press, 2013).

When eternity, which is a first step away from this unity, became further differentiated, deepened its own self-consciousness, then something else appeared, Urizen.[9] When Urizen became self-conscious and could look at himself, he became subject and object, for that is what self-consciousness means. I cannot be self-conscious if I am not aware of myself as subject and, in some sense, as object. When this happened, struggle appeared, for always struggle is always implicit in the very character of self-consciousness. At the same moment that you divide into subject and object, there is always something that tries to reduce subject and object to the original unity. It is the difference between the expression "subject and object" [and] "self-consciousness." That sort of division and the wholeness out of which it comes, that makes for the struggle. Now man has one of those eternals, and man became involved in eternity because long since [he said] "I am" and as soon as he did that he became involved. The same process happened. Man then became more and more differentiated into various aspects of self-consciousness. Then all of the problems that arise between will-to-wholeness, the will-to-unity, and the separateness that is expressed in self-consciousness became a part of man's struggle.

In applying this principle to man, Blake breaks it down further in terms of what he called "specters" and "illuminations." Now the specter[s] are not what is generally thought of by some people. The specters[10] are not evil things as we think of evil things. The specters represent reason, the formal logical processes of mind. The specters represent law and order, regulation, the projection into experience of rationale. The illuminations represent the expression of the deep original, fontal movement of the

---

9. Urizen, one of the central figures in Blake's mythology, symbolizes human reason, which for Blake was equivalent to repression and limitation, the aspect of the divine, which, when fallen, becomes Satan. Urizen appears in *The Book of Urizen* (1794) and the posthumously published *The Four Zoas* (1807), and many other of Blake's works. Urizen rebelled against the other Zoas and eternals, and was forced into a physical form by Los, the representation of the creative imagination. Urizen creates empire, institutes slavery, and institutes the Synagogue of Satan to condemn Jesus; but his religion falls, he loses his physical form, becomes the abominable Dragon, and then eventually repents. There are strong parallels between Urizen and the course of the Satan in Milton's *Paradise Lost*.

10. Specters, in Blake's mythology, represent the rational power of divided man, and they become identified with self-centered selfishness.

Spirit.[11] It is the conflict between good and evil, this dualism, that is a part of the theology of most religions and a part of the ethics of most civilians and societies. In Blake it becomes another kind of struggle; it becomes a struggle between freedom and no-freedom, between the spontaneous expression of the spirit and the discipline that comes from orderly process as expressed in law, in regulations, in the established order, in social patterns, all of those things by which man claims to be a civilized human creature. Therefore, Blake then finds that he is of necessity, because of his deeper orientation to his illuminations and to his specters, opposed to law, to order, to all of the regulations of the codes of morality and the codes of ethics. This is what the specter has done to the mind and the spirit of man, for every time you get a law you curb something. Every time you get a regulation, a thou-shalt-not, you repressed something. It is small wonder then that at one period of his life he gave refuge to Tom Paine,[12] and all sorts of things. The logic of what he worked out from within the context of his mysticism made him an anarchist. It poses a very interesting problem, for when he applies his insight to morality, you see what he gets. All society's regulations are repressive. There is no external, other than self-reference, by which man should be bound. Therefore, Blake stood over against the orderly, rational process of the eighteenth-reaching-into-the-nineteenth century against which he was in interesting and consistent and spiritual revolt.

Now let us push it just a little further, and then we will pull it together. If man, going back a little, is one of the eternals and there is no basic distinction in the eternals and although eternals are one, then if that is true creation, the existence and separateness and so forth represent the fall of

---

11. The illuminations are the feminine part of Man, which Blake sees as bisexual, with its parts to be reunited with their opposites in eternity.

12. Thomas Paine (1737–1809), the English-born revolutionary, arrived in Pennsylvania in 1774, and soon became a leading pamphleteer for the patriot cause, most notably in *Common Sense* (1776). Paine returned to England around 1787, though the prime minister, William Pitt the Younger, thought him a dangerous radical, and indicted him for seditious libel. He escaped to France before his arrest, though he was arrested in Paris during the Terror, and narrowly escaped execution. He returned to the United States in 1802. It was during his years in London in the late 1780s and early 1790s that Paine and Blake met, and Blake played a role in helping to see *The Rights of Man* (1792) to publication, though the story that Blake provided him shelter is likely apocryphal.

man from his original unity; then it means that man is involved on the inside of everything that is creation. Let us say it again. Man is one of the eternals, you see, but remember that all of the eternals are just one eternal. Now when man, the eternal, broke away from the other eternals which are one eternal, he was still one eternal, even though by saying "I exist" he falls from the unity; but the essence of what he is as one of the eternals remains intact. Therefore nothing that man can do, nothing that any individual can do, is really involved in this inner quality, so that any doctrine of sin that arises from it is always external to man, according to Blake, because the only thing that can get to him is something that has its origin in man the eternal. Everything else is outside of him. This is a very deadly doctrine.

Now, everything that is created in the world including human beings, animals, rocks, grass, sand, everything that is created, if you try to get behind a visible to the invisible—remember the double vision again—always you get behind that invisible to another invisible, behind that to another, until at last you come upon the eternal essence, one of the eternals. Therefore, man is the roar of the lion; man is the song of the nightingale; man is the grass; man is the stone; man is the sand which is the gray hair of the earth. Man is all of that. Therefore, he can't be restored, he can't recover from his fall until all of his life—rocks, trees, men, birds, flowers, snakes, scorpions, everything—is one. Do you see what that means? When I look at you I do not see you. Your name is an externality, your features are external, even your little world of thinking is external. When I see you, when I look through the visible to the invisible, I come upon what? I come upon the same essence that is I. When in my behavior I deal with you on that theory then the brotherhood becomes but the human expression of the basic underlying eternal unity that connects all creation. It is tremendous. When I work for brotherhood I am trying to reduce the self-consciousness to zero.

How then are men redeemed from this fall? They are redeemed, says Blake, by Jesus Christ, one of the eternals also. How does the redemption take place? When Jesus Christ, says Blake, became the divine human, then he provided a for-instance for all people to shoot at. He says, "Now you don't have to give yourselves over to your specters, you don't have to do what you are doing. I came through just as you did, and with me and the emanations, the expression of what Blake calls the "original desires of the eternal" is manifest in all of my emanations.[13] Now you can do it. As Blake says it, Jesus Christ took from man his alibis. That is all.

Now how do you work out redemption? Every time I sacrifice my ego—very interesting for the ego is the thing that did it, [said] "I exist," broke away from the eternal—every time I sacrifice that I get closer to the original increment. So when I love you, and because of my love for you, I must relax some crucial and important aspect of my self-regarding impulses. When I sacrifice on behalf of the sick birds or the dog with the broken leg, when I withhold my will to destroy the ant or the rat, says Blake, I sacrifice more and more of my ego, which is the way by which I can come home and disrobe myself of self-consciousness and be the eternal as I was originally. Therefore, all of life becomes a process by which I overcome all the barriers that separate me from you.

Eugene Debs long ago said it in a very simple, almost naïve way: "While there is a lower class I am in it, while there is a criminal element I am of it, while there is a man in jail I am not free."[14] Same thing:

> If I knew you and you knew me
> And each of us could clearly see
> > By inner light divine
> > The meaning of your life and mine,
> I am sure that we would differ less
> And clasp our hand in friendliness
> > If I knew you and you knew me. [15]

Someone else puts it another way:

> Ere the kingdom neath the skies
> Often he falls, yet falls to rise,

---

13. That is to say, for Blake, one's desires, rather than one's ability to reason, connect an individual to the eternal.

14. This is one of Thurman's favorite statements, told by Eugene V. Debs (1856–1926) to the judge who sentenced him to ten years in prison in 1918 for his opposition to World War I.

15. "If I Knew You and You Knew Me," by Nixon Waterman (1859–1944), an American poet and editor.

> Stumbling, bleeding, beaten back,
> Holding still to the upward track,
> Playing his part in creation's plan,
> God-like in image; this is man.[16]

Blake would add: God-like in image: this is everything. So I walk the earth with reverence and with great dignity, knocking at every door in order that I might be released from the things that bind me and shut me off from all others, and that is achieved, and the Judgment Day, in Blake's language, has come to pass, and the original harmony of the eternals is restored.

That is it. Part of it anyway.

---

16. A poem frequently cited by Thurman, from an anonymous source, see Robert Scott and William C. Stiles, eds., *Cyclopedia of Illustrations for Public Speakers* (New York: Funk & Wagnalls, 1911), 446.

Lao-Tse

19 April 1953
Fellowship Church

In this sermon, Thurman discusses Lao-Tse and the main tenet of Taoism (or Daoism), the seeking of Dao, or "the Way."[1] Thurman's exposition is less interested in the details of Taoism as a Chinese religion and religious philosophy than in making the case for Taoism as an authentically Chinese form of mysticism. For Thurman, "all the mystics are saying the same thing," rejecting intermediaries and institutional impositions between the mystic and God. They find God through "renunciation, detachment ... withdrawal, the reduction of fever."[2] Although Taoism, through its doctrine of "non-action," would seem to be a doctrine of complete passivity, Thurman argues that mystic detachment is less a retreat from the world than a recognition that rather than being "overwhelmed by the mass attack of the tyranny of detail," the mystic realizes that the individual cannot "make a quantitative impression on infinity" but is concerned with "finding where your center is and sticking with it," and thereby changing themselves and their world.

Today I'm somewhat embarrassed we have with us a man who has spent a quarter of a century in China and knows more than in two

---

1. Thurman previously spoke on Lao-Tse, "Men Who Have Walked with God: Lao-Tse," 30 April 1950.
2. The belief that all mystics share a common belief system was central to the emergence of mysticism as a subject of scholarly research in the late nineteenth century. Some recent scholars have argued that this approach underestimates the extent to which mysticism can only be understood within the context of specific and noncongruent religious cultures; see Steven V. Katz, "Introduction," *Comparative Mysticism: An Anthology of Original Sources* (New York: Oxford University Press, 2013), 2–23.

lifetimes I shall learn.[3] But it is very interesting to remind you that one of the simple guides that I have had all of my life, particularly since I have been preaching, is this: I assume always that in any audience of any kind to which I am speaking that there is at least one person in the audience who knows more about what I am talking about than I do. And it has been a wonderful thing, and it has saved me much—and that keeps me in the presence of authentic authorities from being self-conscious.

The fundamental proposition on which we are working during these days is this: That the mystic affirms that God is the Creator of life totally, and that every living thing is a manifestation of that creativity; and deep within the structure of every living thing is a core of reality which is in essence one with that out of which all of life comes. As far as human life is concerned, the mystic says, in language that is religious, that deep within the human spirit there is God. Not a manifestation of God but that which is God. Therefore he who seeks God may find him within; there is a door that no man can shut, and that door is deep within the human spirit. In the last analysis all intermediaries, all things which lead men to God, are not ultimately required in order that men may find God. And that is why the mystic needs no intermediary; he needs no symbol because the thing itself is in his heart, and "it is closer than breathing, it is nearer than hands and feet."[4] Yet, it is rather interesting, isn't it, that in the Christian religion, the greatest movement of mysticism has come out of the Roman Catholic Church, which is a paradox, but we shall deal with that when we come to it and we are not to it this morning.

In the period between 1000 BC and AD 100 or 200 every single creative spiritual, ethical, and philosophic movement in human history emerged and became articulate. It is an amazing thing. In the period between 1000 BC and AD 100 or 200, right there in that, all the prophets of Israel, the great upward surge of the creative Spirit of God in Hinduism and in Buddhism, the movement of mysticism and ethics in China, all of the searching wrestling of the Greek philosophers, Jesus of Naza-

---

3. Presumably Thurman is referring to Dryden Phelps (1892–1977), who would soon succeed him as pastor of Fellowship Church. He was a published expert on Chinese religion, having spent the better part of three decades teaching in China prior to the 1949 revolution. See PHWT 4: 73n1.

4. Alfred Lord Tennyson, "The Higher Pantheism" (1869), l. 12.

reth and Paul of Tarsus, all in that period. The implications of that are very far reaching, but you work them out.[5]

It is small wonder then that we find Lao-Tse appearing in the seventh century BC.[6] He is in that period. The great insight which this man had may be summarized in simple words: He affirmed Tao as the Creator of life and the ground of all being, as one who existed before existence, who is without name because he is without category. But inasmuch as all the thinking of the mind has to be done in terms that are spatial in order to talk about it, we must reduce it to some form that is symbolic, even the word itself. Now the insight is rather interesting because it dares to go behind all expressions of life in any form. It is behind the act of creation; it is before any contrast like good and evil, like male and female, right/wrong, light/dark, before any differentiation took place. It is a movement like the movement of absolute motion. It is dynamic without action. It is that out of which everything that is emerges.

Now there is nothing new about that; there is nothing particularly original except originality in its truest sense. And what is that? That anytime an insight becomes my own, then something happens that has never happened in human history before. The insight becomes mine; and if it has never been mine before, then that is new, that's creative, that's original.

Now, I'm not surprised that this notion—it's more than that—this feeling, the mood of the "before beginning," is a part of the heritage of the whole human family because in all of the religions whatever, of whatever kind there is this feeling, this groping after the reproduction of wholeness, of totality, of completeness. The Garden of Eden complete, whole, no contrast, no contradiction, not even the intimations of paradox. All of the harassment of the mind that keeps whipping us toward dreams of Utopias, of Golden Age, of Heaven, it seems to be, all of that

---

5. This simultaneous flowering of transcendental thinking is now often called, following the German philosopher Karl Jaspers (1889–1969), the Axial Age. Jaspers's best-known account, *The Origins and Goal of History* (New Haven, CT: Yale University Press, 1953), was published in English at about the time of Thurman's sermon. but the idea precedes the work of Jaspers.

6. The historicity of Laozi (or Lao-Tse; Wade-Giles transliterations in parentheses), the author of the *Daodejing* (Tao-Te-Ching), is extremely dubious, but some scholars believe he lived in the fourth century BCE, the time when the text of the *Daodejing* emerged; but whether it is the product of a single author is not clear.

stirring seems to be the echo of a previous movement somewhere in the background of human history.[7] Even my private needs for wholeness, I am always trying to become integrated, I am always trying to find myself and then become myself. To be what I am, to do what I see so that the profound conflicts that tear my spirit asunder can be resolved and I will be a whole person. Why do I want that? Why is it a necessity for me and why do I seek it always? It is because my spirit is haunted by a movement in which I participated before I became a house divided against itself? I wonder. At any rate, the first insight of Tao is that here is this ground, this wholeness out of which all separateness came.

Now how does this manifest itself? It manifests itself in a certain quality, and there is a name for that quality: The Tao in action is the way this quality is defined. Wherever there is life manifesting itself, there the Tao is in action; and if I seek to find the Tao, I may find the Tao not only in myself but I may find it in all manifestations by which my life is surrounded. Therefore there must be some method by which I may do this, some technique. And what is the technique? They have a technical name for it, the name escapes my mind for the moment, but it is the Way.[8] And what is the Way, how do you walk in that Way? What is the technique by which the individual in whom Tao is, who is surrounded by manifestations of life in which Tao is, how does the individual become conscious of the Tao-ness that is within him and the Tao-ness that is in these manifestations? What is the method? Renunciation, renunciation, detachment. You'll hear these for the next ten weeks; you'll just hear it over and over again. Detachment, withdrawal, the reduction of fever. Some interpreters say that it is non-action but that is not the way to say it, for when we use the term non-action we think of a certain kind of quietism, a certain kind of passivity; but what he is getting at is that there begins to dawn upon the individual, the seeker, the awareness that what he is seeking really by all of his feverish activity is not to be found in the activities themselves.[9] It is the discovery that you can't make a quantitative impression on infinity. You can't. Values are not to be found by the multiplication of

---

7. Thurman would develop this thesis of the connection between creation myths and utopias in *The Search for Common Ground* (New York: Harper & Row, 1971).

8. Dao is the Chinese word for "the way."

9. Thurman is referring to the Taoist doctrine of *wu wei*, or "non-doing."

function. You can't give yourself over to busyness, business, and find this because you are so concentrated with tensions lest you miss the thing that you seek. It is before your very eyes and you can't see it. Doing, action, functioning, management, participation, here, there, everywhere, being constantly overwhelmed by the mass attack of the tyranny of detail. In the midst of all of this the individual has a sense of being lost and confused because he doesn't have a chance to distill out of some fragment of his experience the Tao that is there, because he can't wait long enough. He grabs it here and he squeezes it hard, and if it doesn't come right out, he has to run over here to get it, over here and over here and over here. All the time what he is looking for he has and doesn't know it. Now when I become aware that I have it, then I stop looking and start being. And that's what he is saying.

And now, one more little word about it. It doesn't mean that there is a withdrawal from participation in life, but it means finding where your center is and sticking with it. And that takes discipline because we are so pulled apart in directions that themselves are so inviting that for many of us to apply this to our own period and our own moment in human history, for many of us have never taken the time to find out where our center is. Have you? How many of us have ever stopped to find out where our center is, what our point of focus is. What are you really trying to do? What is the meaning of all of the activities in which you are engaged? What are you after? If you were able this moment by magic to have the deepest longings of your spirit fulfilled what would they be? Do you know? Do you know? When that time comes as it must come to us all, when one by one our duties end, when one by one our lights go out, when we withdraw from all of the variety of our participations in the functioning and the activities of our living, what will we have left that will be for us the distilled essence of the totality of our endeavoring as human beings? What about it? Or are you so busy, so involved, so frantic, so full of fear, so panicky that you can't hear the pulse of the Tao in you.

When I was in divinity school—and I'm through now—I had a group of adults that met across town at half past ten on Tuesday nights. We would meet from half past ten until twelve, twelve thirty, sometimes one o'clock. Then I would walk the length of Main Street in Rochester, New York, all the way out to the seminary. And one night as I walked along, I kept hearing a noise like flowing water. And I had been wrestling with a little cold and I had taken a lot of quinine by the doctor's orders in that far-off time, and I thought it was a rumbling in my ears. So I said to one of my profs the next day that I had a strange experience at two o'clock in the morning walking down Main Street. And he said, "Oh no, it wasn't the rumbling in your ear at all." He said, "Main Street is built over a canal that connects the Genesee River[10] or some river with something else, and all during the day there is so much traffic—streetcars, automobiles, blowing of horns—that you can't hear this canal flowing, but late at night when there is no traffic then there comes rumbling up out of the bowels of Main Street this movement of sound.[11] It is there all of the time. That's the Tao. There is so much noise in us, so much movement that we can't hear the movement of the Tao and we cannot let it spill over into us at various levels of our awareness and our division that it might bring to all of that which is divided, a wholeness; to that which is tempest-tossed, a calmness; to that which is despairing, hope. Whether it be Tao or whether it be the Demiurge,[12] whether it be the eternal fire,[13] whether it be the God of Abraham, Isaac, and Jacob, or whether it be the thought of Jesus Christ, all the mystics are saying the same thing: "Thou hast made us for Thyself and our souls are restless 'til they find their rest in Thee."[14] That is the message.

---

10. Thurman was correct. It was the Genesee River.

11. Thurman had been teaching a Bible study class for women at the Colored YWCA. Because most of the women were maids or domestics and were not free until their duties for the day were complete, the class began late in the evening; see Peter Eisenstadt, *Against the Hounds of Hell: A Life of Howard Thurman* (Charlottesville: University of Virginia Press, 2021), 77.

12. In Plato and Platonism, the demiurge is the creator of the physical universe. In many schools of Gnostic thought, the demiurge is malevolent, and in opposition to the higher unknowable God.

13. A religious idea central to Zoroastrianism.

14. St. Augustine, *Confessions* 1.1.

Buddha

3 May 1953
Fellowship Church

Thurman's attitudes toward Buddhism, as reflected in this sermon, were complex. He admired Buddhism's emphasis on meditation.[1] He distrusted Buddhist doctrines that maintained that "the self has no enduring value or significance," and that as a result "all of life is a mechanical, materialistic operation" in which "there is no provision made for any creative operation upon the logic of events." In the previous week's sermon on Brahman mysticism, not printed in this volume, Thurman claimed that the Brahman mystics believed that they were "above good and above evil" because they were "involved in union with the world soul, which union was the only reality and anything else was an unreality."[2] But since everyone, after their death, is in "perpetual communion with the world soul" that meant "that what you do while you are living has made no difference," and "then the religious experience cannot sustain any kind of moral or ethical enterprise."

To avoid this consequence, Thurman argues, Brahmans used the idea of reincarnation to differentiate individual fates. But Brahman mystics tied these doctrines to specific rituals and ceremonials and confined their attention to those in their own elite caste. What happens, asked Thurman, "to the masses of people who can't do that, who can't solve the problem in that way, what happens to them?" This, says Thurman, is what the Buddha tried to answer. The answer was stark. All life is suffering, and "the root of it is desire." Desire is rooted, grounded in the life process itself. The end of all of life is "to arrive at a point that is beyond significance, beyond feeling, beyond desire." Moving toward this goal was open to everyone, regardless of their caste background. But as with Brahman mysticism, Thurman worried that

---

1. Thurman had previously spoken on Buddhism, "Men Who Have Walked with God: Buddha," Fellowship Church, May 1950.
2. "Men Who Have Walked with God III: Brahman Mystics," 26 April 1953.

this made individual action unimportant and insignificant. He holds out the possibility, against Buddhism, pointing to Jesus, and perhaps the Buddha himself, that "one man with one mind can stand over against the logic even of human history and hold his creative power at dead center over this logical stuff until a new law moves out of him and invades the stuff of human history." This was essentially what Gandhi told Thurman about his mission.[3]

At the same time, though he worried about the implications of the Buddhist doctrine that "you cannot be free until you are free of the necessity even of being yourself," he saw affinities between his understanding of nonviolence, as expounded in Jesus and the Disinherited *and elsewhere. The de-emphasis on the self properly placed attention on the "event, the act and its results." It is not enough to oppose evil in one's heart; one must take action. Thurman concluded that "after all these centuries we still do not dare try the thing" that the Buddha suggested: "To make an attack on moral disorder in the world by the purification of one's own life on the theory and in the faith that something redemptive in character can be radiated from that." A central paradox of Buddhism for Thurman is that purifying one's life and the elimination of self is a recognition of the "responsibility to radiate a quality of living that will influence the minds, the thinking, and the processes of the people around me."*

Today we are continuing our series. Just very simple and limited aspects of Buddhism.[4]

Buddha was a seeker.[5] He wanted to find a solution to the problem of human existence. And I suppose in that sense we are all seekers, aren't we? Of course, we do not define our quest in such lofty terms, but ultimately what we are after is the final solution to the riddle of our private existence.

---

3. See the discussion between Thurman and Gandhi in PHWT 1: 335–36.
4. Like the other sermons in this series on topics in Eastern religion, Thurman's account of Buddhism is rather general, avoiding citation of specific texts, schools of Buddhist thought or practice, or the historical development of the religion.
5. Siddhartha Gautama, usually known as the Buddha (or the "enlightened one"), lived in northeastern India between the sixth and fourth centuries BCE.

There are many stories about Buddha and you may know more of them than I do, but let us cut through all that the devotion and the imagination and the inspired response of millions of human beings have given to this creative and moving spirit who seems in himself to be so completely one with what he claims to have found that when his worshipers contemplate his life they think of him as the only God worthy of worship. He wanted to know the answer to human suffering. Everywhere he looked around him in the world he saw men who were suffering. Young people were getting older, old people were getting older; no man escaped old age if he continued to live, and old age brought with it the disintegration of powers of body and mind. And it seemed, as contrasted with the glory and the wonder and the beauty of youth, to be tragedy. He saw around him men who were hungry and who could find no food to eat, and the living of their lives on the basis of the provisions that were available to them seemed to him, and perhaps to them, to be an increasing nightmare without reason and without tenderness. He saw people die. "One by one the duties end, one by one the lights go out. The tallest mountain must crumble, the strongest beam must break, the wisest man withers like a plant: death everywhere riding on all the winds."[6] What is there about the nature of human existence that makes of all of life a breeding ground for anguish of spirit? That was his problem. He set out to find it. If I can get rid of my flesh, if I can get rid of the persistent demands of my body, if somehow I can detach myself from my time-space involvement then I can be free of this thing which is responsible for all of the suffering of life and therefore is responsible for life itself. In his thinking it seemed that life and suffering were synonymous, and here he broke with the Brahmanic mystics, for the Brahmanic mystics recognized that life was made up of that which was good and that which is evil, that life is a combination of the positive and the negative, of joy and sorrow, of hope and despair; and therefore the devout Brahman felt that if he could, by ecstasy, lift himself above the commonplace then he would be beyond good and evil, and

---

6. This is a composite quotation. The first sentence is from James Lane Allen, *A Kentucky Tale of the Olden Time* (Philadelphia: J. B. Lippincott, 1893), 216. The second sentence is from James Legge's translation of *The Chinese Classics, Vol. 1* (Hong Kong and London: James Trubner, 1861), 87, describing a quotation from an uncited source on Confucius's recognition of his impending death.

only those who were not able to do that would be caught in the agonizing grapple of the tensions between good and evil. But for Gautama life is evil because life has desire, life means desire, and it is of the nature of desire that it can never be fulfilled. Very interesting isn't it? When I got there I said, "Well, the thing that I want I will find, yeah." But when I got there it wasn't there; it was somewhere else. And then when I got to that other place that I had located, then it wasn't there. "All experience is an arch where through gleams an untraveled world whose margin fades forever and forever when I move."[7] The fight would never be over, no not even in death. Isn't that human experience? That's what he says anyway.

Inasmuch as it is true in his thinking that you cannot fulfill desire, then desire must be attacked in a more fundamental manner. Desire must be rooted out. But you cannot root out desire unless somehow you are able to destroy in the human spirit the will to live. And the will to live is intimately a part of the love of life.

One of his disciples said to him when he was talking about nirvana and how nirvana is bliss, and he said, "But if nirvana is bliss then that means that you are feeling something, you are enjoying something." And he said, "No, nirvana is bliss because it is bliss to be rid completely of all desire."

Now let's look at this. The root of human suffering is desire. Desire is rooted, grounded in the life process itself. The end of all of life in terms of its most significance is to arrive at a point where significance is irrelevant; to arrive at a point that is beyond significance, beyond feeling, beyond desire.

In Washington, DC, in the old part of the Rock Creek Cemetery, there is a statue built by Saint-Gaudens, a statue built as a memorial to the wife of Henry Adams. You may remember that in one of the Galsworthy novels published after his death there is a long description of this member of the Forsythe family who lands in Washington and he sits in front of this statue and makes a very important discovery about the meaning of human existence.[8] Well, very often during the years that I lived in Wash-

---

7. "Yet all experience is an arch wherethro'/Gleams that untravell'd world whose margin fades" (Alfred Lord Tennyson, "Ulysses" [1842], ll. 19–20).

8. John Galsworthy, *Two Forsythe Interludes: A Silent Wooing, Passers By* (New York: Charles Scribners, 1928), 34.

ington, I would go out to Rock Creek Cemetery. And every visitor who came to preach in the University Chapel, I arranged to take him out there sometimes before the service because it was very helpful in many ways. There is a woman seated in a chair, her body is draped with a huge bit of greenish bronze coming over her face and covering everything except a hand, the hands. Her cheek is resting on the hand and the elbow is leaning on the arm of the seat and she is looking straight ahead. And as you look at her, you see that every tear that was in her has been cried out, that there is nothing left that can register awareness. She is beyond all tension, beyond all struggle, beyond all the contradictions of life and she has landed out there somewhere. And they call that statue "Nirvana."[9]

Now, the meaning of what Buddha found after going through all, the meaning of what Buddha found after going through all of the varied experiences of life, after starving himself to death, almost to death, running the whole gamut of flagellation and reduction of the self, he found that he couldn't do it that way. That he couldn't by thinking it through do it; he couldn't by meditating do it; the only thing he could do was—well, he didn't know. It is very interesting. He didn't know. He didn't know what he could do. He could wait. He could wait and see if he could get still enough inside, but [this is not] the stillness of no activity altogether, but it is more like the stillness of absolute motion,[10] a stillness that is so utterly dynamic that it isn't activity at all. It's very interesting. I can't put it into words, but when this happened to him then he had illumination. And what was illumination? And you see I am trying to talk about it from the outside of my mind and I can't do it. Illumination, whatever illumination was, it freed him of all of the necessities of existence. He

---

9. The writer and historian Henry Adams (1838–1918) commissioned Augustus Saint-Gaudens (1848–1907) to create a sculpture on the tomb of his wife, Marian "Clover" Hooper Adams (1843–1885), who had taken her own life. Completed in 1891, it was modeled on the Japanese Buddhist deity Kannon, the bodhisattva of compassion. Commonly called "Grief," it was a favorite statue of Thurman, who often took visiting preachers at Howard University to view it (WHAH 91–92).

10. Thurman used the same phrase to describe the 1963 March on Washington, writing a friend, "You should have been in Washington on August 28. Nothing like has ever happened in the history of our country. I was one of 200,000 people sharing a moment that contained all time and all experience, when everything was moving and everything was standing still, a moment that had in it the stillness of absolute motion" (cited in Eisenstadt, *Against the Hounds of Hell*, 320).

preached about it afterwards for suddenly it seemed to him that he had arrived at a place at which it was up to him to go forward, to come back and pick up life or go on beyond, but not go on beyond as Buddha but go on beyond the self and the limitations of the self.

Now, naturally when he had that experience, he had to give a blueprint. His disciples wanted to know how do you do it, and he wanted to share it so we get a lot of instructions, techniques: the eightfold path, right speech, right thinking, right living, right meditation, etc.[11] But it is quite possible to follow all of the steps of the eightfold path and not get it.

Now what is the bearing of all of this in his life in terms of his ethic and his—and the crucial problem of the masses of people, for it is with that point that we are concerned? You remember—I will have to take an extra minute this morning—when we were discussing the whole doctrine of reincarnation and the insistence that the souls became involved in the deeds that we do, and the deeds affected the quality of the soul, and therefore the soul had to get its purification. And if it meant coming back again and again and again and again because the theory of time upon which we were operating is a circular theory of time. You cannot be free until you are free of the necessity even of being yourself. And it is so difficult for us in our culture and civilization to grapple with that because all of our emphasis is upon self-realization, of coming to oneself. What we are all striving to do sometime is to say with reference to something, "I did it. I did it." And a whole school of psychology has developed around the idea of the necessity for taking personal responsibility for your individual actions.[12] The self—coming to one's self is defined in all of these various ways. But here is the reverse of that. Buddha insists that the self has no enduring value or significance; that the only thing that endures is the event, the act, and its results. Long before John Watson worked on behaviorism at Hopkins University, here is behaviorism, hundreds of years before.[13] What is it that counts? The deed. And each deed carries its

---

11. The eightfold path is a central Buddhist doctrine.
12. Thurman is probably thinking of the school of individual psychology associated with the theories of the Viennese psychologist Alfred Adler (1870–1937).
13. John B. Watson (1878–1958), the American psychologist who maintained in his theory of behaviorism that our identity is a product of our external stimuli rather than a product of a coherent, interior self.

own value, its own merit, its own judgment, its own logic. The self is not important in terms of the effect of the deed on the self. So that when one dies—one goes through a sort of opening, a little place, just big enough for the self to get through but not big enough for all these events to get through, so they are left outside as you would leave your clothes outside, but when you go in, you find that you didn't do your work well and you must come back. There is only one way that you can come back and that is right back through that same place and pick up what you left at the door. The only way you can get rid of that is to finally to arrive at a place that there is nothing left at the door and then you are free. [This is] the event.

Now, you see, you see what that means in terms of human history? It is an amazing thing that all of human life is involved in the operation of law, the operation of logic, the operation of antecedent, consequence, reaping, sowing, and there is no provision made for any creative operation upon the logic of events. If I want to alter the history of the world, there is only one way by which it can be altered in this pattern of thought and that is to alter the events which in turn will influence the consequence. It is interesting because an aspect of this appears in the thought of Jesus; do you remember? He pictures the end of human history when all the people in the world will come before the great judgment. And what is interesting about the judgment is not the judge and what he has to say—keep the sheep on the right the goats on the left—but what determines whether you are a sheep or a goat?[14] The judge? No. The event, the event. I was sick and you didn't come to see me. I was in prison and you didn't visit me etc. The history of the individual's life became his judgment.

Now long before Jesus of Nazareth appears here is a man wrestling with that same problem. It is not a complete answer, and I don't have time now to deal with it, because it makes all of life a mechanical, materialistic operation. And it confines the activities of the human spirit within the starkest kind of determinism, and I don't think that life is like that altogether. I think there is always a margin in which it is possible for the creative human spirit to elect an alternative that violates even the logic of events. One man with one mind can stand over against the logic even of human history and hold his creative power at dead center over this logi-

---

14. Matthew 25:31–46.

cal stuff until a new law moves out of him and invades the stuff of human history. And that is why I think life is good rather than evil, because it has that possibility.

Now I know I should stop, but if you will just bear with me for two more minutes.

I am concerned, at one more step here, about the ethic that is involved in this. You remember—no you don't—when we talked about the Jainists I said that they did not project this doctrine of ahimsa about which Mahatma Gandhi talks so much because they wanted to do something positive. They said, "Thou shalt not kill," not because of the respect that they had for the life that would be destroyed, but "thou shall not kill" because if I kill then I defile myself. And it is because I do not wish to become contaminated that I will not kill you. Not because I love you or don't love you, but I don't want to get dirty so I will not kill you. That's very nice of me.[15]

Now the ethic that is a derivative from the discovery of Buddha is the ethic of self-purification, which is the next creative step from this position that the Jainists disclose. Self-purification. I get rid of desire, and in ridding myself of desire through processes that are familiar to the Buddhists I purify myself. But this is the wonderfully glorious thing about his insight. He discovered that if an individual becomes sufficiently pure in his life that the purity of his life radiates automatically without the movement of his will even. The purity of his life radiates a quality that is moral in character, that affects the lives of other people. And by so doing, you see, he introduces a life-affirming concept into a position which basically is life-denying. For, you see, if I get rid of the self and so forth and self-purification, that is withdrawal, that is life-denying; that is not life-affirming. And the logic of that position, you see, is to withdraw, [and those who] come in touch with that radiation find themselves affected by the quality of my purity. "Therefore," he said, "the responsibility of the individual becomes a double responsibility. I will purify myself that I may get from under the necessities of existence. But in the purification of

---

15. Jainism is an ancient Indian religion, dating from the fifth century BCE, that placed a great emphasis on non-violence and ascetic practices. The Jainist doctrine of ahimsa, and the Jainist worldview in general, as Thurman notes, was a major influence on Mahatma Gandhi.

myself I recognize the responsibility to radiate a quality of living that will influence the minds, the thinking, and the processes of the people around me." And his great contribution to ethics is at that point he defines direct action in terms that have to do with the inner purity of the life. And after all these centuries we still do not dare try the thing that he suggested: to make an attack on moral disorder in the world by the purification of one's own life on the theory and in the faith that something redemptive in character can be radiated from that. And until we test that, how dare we set up our faith, whatever it may be, with arrogance and pride and look with judgment upon the face of the Buddha.

Plotinus

10 May 1953
Fellowship Church

The time is the third quarter of the third century AD. The city is the imperial city of Rome. The crumbling empire is in evidence on every hand. The vital and dynamic energized barbarians are pushing over the frontier making sporadic raids, dipping always more deeply into the heart of the empire. Plague is everywhere. Men and women are dying because of the working of some invisible something. The emperors lose their thrones quickly, and new emperors come on the throne; the throne itself is in a tilted place. And no one who sits there can find equilibrium because the grounds upon which the whole empire rests are now disintegrating. And into this city, on the outskirts, is a little community of people. The leader, the teacher, is Plotinus. It is the only calm spot in the Greek and Roman world, as it seems.[1]

So opens a 1961 sermon by Thurman on one of his favorite mystics, Plotinus. Like the subject of the next sermon in "Men Who Have Walked with God" series, St. Augustine, Plotinus was born into the faltering political and social realities of the late Roman Empire. But unlike Augustine, Plotinus seems to have had little interest in thinking about the fate of empires or what sort of civic and religious structures might replace Rome. Plotinus would seem to be a pure example of a "negation mystic," with a totally inward focus. But that is not how Thurman saw him. In his own way, Thurman told his audience, Plotinus used his mysticism not to remove himself from the mass of humanity but to insinuate himself within it, and create a place of calm for himself

---

1. HT, "Plotinus: The Inward Journey" (26 November 1961), in Folder 11, Box 14, HTC, Boston University.

and others at a time of trouble. "All the little children liked him"; and when average people spoke to Plotinus about their troubles, "whatever the difficulty was just didn't seem quite as difficult after talking with Plotinus as it did before."

Plotinus could accomplish this because of, and not despite, his forbiddingly complex mystical and metaphysical system, which Thurman describes in considerable detail, the journey of the individual soul to reunite with its severed half on the path to true self-realization and divine union. For Thurman, Plotinus realized that the soul was "symbolic of the movement of the spirit of God in the life of man," and the realization that "all of life, all creation was in God," and "all created things, all time-space expressions, all of these are in God."

Evidently there were some in Fellowship Church who wondered about the need for a sermon series on mystics and why Thurman was "spending so much time talking about these people that nobody has ever heard about and they don't have anything to do with what we are about." He understood the frustration, but he was convinced that exposure to the great mystics, with their own personal mythologies and theologies, was necessary, because there was "something in human experience that seems to me to be cumulative," a "wisdom in the human spirit that is greater than the particular wisdom of the particular man" and "a vitality that is greater than my vitality or your vitality." This can inspire us to find our own individual ways to demonstrate the truth "that apart from man's active awareness of the presence of the living God in his life he cannot expect to find either meaningful living or significant living." And if the theology of Plotinus seems esoteric, available to only a handful of adepts, its essence, and that of the other great mystics, was "available to any man anywhere at any moment in any age whether his is rich or poor, ugly or beautiful, educated or illiterate, sophisticated or simple, it makes no difference." Without knowing something of Plotinus and the other great mystics, an individual might not know how to understand or react to that moment when they are "visited, always temporarily, by a surging something that sweeps him beyond the furthest rim of human thought and then it turns him loose and he says, 'Haaaah,' and drops back into himself or herself."

Let us continue our series by making a great leap ahead and thinking together with you about Plotinus.[2] Some of you have very gently and deftly raised the question with me as to why are we spending so much time talking about these people that nobody has ever heard about and they don't have anything to do with what we are about. And I confess to you that I can understand out of what source of frustration that expression arises, but as I have said to some of you personally, we are all of us concerned about trying to find somehow the clue to living so that as the years unfold for us, living for us will be increasingly a meaningful and deeply satisfying experience. And it is the insight of men through the ages, which insight is effectively dramatized in certain of these individuals, that apart from man's active awareness of the presence of the living God in his life he cannot expect to find either meaningful living or significant living. And it isn't as if human life or the individual's life took place in isolation and everyman would have to go through all of the experiences through which men before him went. But there is something in human experience that seems to me, for lack of a better term, that seems to me to be cumulative. There is a wisdom in the human spirit that is greater than the particular wisdom of the particular man, however wise and intelligent and profound he may be. There is a vitality that is greater than my vitality or your vitality; there is a strength greater than my strength or your strength. And that element, that dimension of life has been at work in the life of man through all these years: it has built up a kind of momentum, a kind of backlog of experience, of knowledge, yes, and of wisdom upon which any individual may draw whether or not he understands the language, whether or not he is a part of the culture. It has nothing to do with anything that is literate. It has everything to do with the push of life in which all living things have shared. And wherever I touch life I draw on that. And I may not be able to recognize it.

---

2. Plotinus (205–271 CE) was born in Lycopolis, Egypt (in the Nile Delta region). He studied philosophy in Alexandria. After attaching himself to Emperor Gordian III's failed invasion of Persia in 243, supposedly out of an interest in studying Persian and Indian philosophy he moved to Rome, where he spent the rest of his life. He is considered the founder of the Neoplatonic school of ancient philosophy, which developed the metaphysical monism inherent in the work of Plato. His work is preserved in his treatises known as the *Enneads*. See Plotinus, *The Enneads* (ed. Lloyd P. Gerson et al.; Cambridge, UK: Cambridge University Press, 2018).

I remember the first time I studied a little of Greek philosophy and ran into Socrates and Plato, now and then certain things became clear in their words and with a great sense of freedom and with no sense of modesty whatsoever I felt that, "why I've been thinking that way a long time." You know, "I know what he is talking about."[3] And I'd never heard of Socrates or Plato or the Greeks, except the men who ran the restaurant downtown. I mean I had no [idea] that all that the human spirit has accumulated, all that has been breathed through it by the living breath of the living God is available to any man anywhere at any moment in any age whether he is rich or poor, ugly or beautiful, educated or illiterate, sophisticated or simple, it makes no difference. That's what these men are talking about. And that is why there are moments when you related to what they are saying and feeling in ways that have nothing to do with the formal discursive parts of your mind. And under stress—well, all this isn't Plotinus. Let's just get to Plotinus, the time is just running.

Plotinus came into the world about the third century AD. He was the flowering of this wonderfully creative process that had been going on in human history that we think of now in terms of Greek philosophy. He was the mystic: the mystic of the spirit. He was a different kind of mystic from Plato. Plato was an intellectual mystic, but Plotinus was—I wish I could have known him. All the little children liked him. They enjoyed talking to him; he related himself to them at the points of their understanding. He became the custodian of a garden variety of non-descript children and brooded over them. People sought him out to tell him their troubles. They felt if they could talk to Plotinus, whatever the difficulty was just didn't seem quite as difficult after talking with Plotinus as it did before. He, apparently, he loved people, and people loved him. They responded to him and he responded to them.[4] That was Plotinus; the man walking through Greek life spreading radiation and beauty and kindness.

---

3. Thurman's first exposure to Greek philosophy was in the summer of 1922, when he stayed with an uncle in Cleveland. Preparing for a summer class in philosophy at Columbia University, he went to a local library, telling the librarian, "I have never read a book on philosophy. Can you help me?" Most of his reading was in Greek philosophy (WHAH 43–44).

4. Almost all we know about the life of Plotinus is contained in his pupil Porphyry's (234–305) *Life of Plotinus*. See M. J. Edwards, *Neoplatonic Saints: The Lives of Plotinus and Proclus by Their Students* (Liverpool: Liverpool University Press, 2000).

What a wonderful thing. But he had a secret, and it is about his secret that we want to talk for the remaining minutes.

Plotinus felt, taught, thought that all of life, all creation was in God. Now mark you, these other men up to this time, and we will see how they move subsequently, were sure that God was in the world, you see, and that wherever you touched any form of matter, somewhere locked up in it was spirit. But Plotinus says that all over the world, all created things, all time-space expressions, all of these are in God; that God surrounds, envelops, encloses matter, things, vicissitudes, change, shifts.

Now, the soul, and it is important in getting the clue of his insight to his secret to deal primarily with his interpretation of the soul of man. The soul of man is split. Well that's not the best way to put it. Let me see. Well, let me talk about it, and then I'll get the phrase. The soul of man, when man is born, a part of his soul is left in the divine sphere. Bear in mind now some of the other minds who dealt with this same problem, that when man is created a part of his soul is left up here and part comes down and participates in creation. But all of the soul of the individual is not in the individual's body; a part of it is left.

Now the part that is in the body, because it is in the body and is involved in all the appetites and so forth and so on of the body, its awareness as a soul becomes dimmer and dimmer. It's like a new pair of shoes. The first time you put them on they are scuff free, they show no marks of anything from walking; but the longer you wear them the less new they seem to be. He said, that's it, the soul gets dim and a little more dim and more dim as it is removed in its awareness, and this may not have anything to do with time, bear in mind, as it is removed from its awareness of its origin and the other part of it.

Now, he says that in order for the soul to become aware of its self, aware of itself—to itself, that's the phrase that Jesus uses[5]—when the soul, says Plotinus, comes to itself then immediately it becomes aware of the part of itself that it left in what Plotinus calls the "divine sphere," and a movement begins. The two parts of the soul gravitate towards each other. So, it is in Plotinus that we get the double movement of the spirit, moving down this way and moving up this way. It finds its classi-

---

5. Thurman is no doubt referring to the Parable of the Prodigal Son, Luke 15:17.

cal expression finally in Christianity, for Plotinus belonged to the school that influenced the church fathers, and Augustine bore heavily upon it, drew heavily upon him.[6] By the time this concept, this moving down and moving up, gets into the Christian movement, we get the seeking God and the responding individual; we get the figure, for instance, who seeks the lost sheep and the bleating lost sheep crying for the shepherd—the double movement.[7] We get it in Francis Thompson's "Hound of Heaven" seeking: the relentless divine nemesis tracking the human soul—stalking it.[8] And yet at the same time the movement of the human soul, the pull toward something that is more than it now experiences, more than it now knows, more than it now understands. And we have all felt that, haven't we? There is something, there is something in me that reaches for more than anything that I know; there is a hunger in me for something that all that I know and have and taste and feel and experience cannot quite satisfy. That is what Plotinus is talking about. Not so far-fetched after all, is it?

Now when the heart, when the soul comes to itself and makes its contact, this movement when the soul gets together with itself—homecoming—in that moment the soul becomes aware of what Plotinus calls the universal soul, what Emerson called the over-soul.[9] He becomes aware of it. And in that awareness a very interesting thing happens. In that aware-

---

6. In "Plotinus: The Inward Journey," Thurman states that Plotinus was a greater influence on the thought of St Augustine than anyone besides Jesus and Paul, and that his impact on "the whole floodtide of the Christian faith" was "in a manner that is almost beyond belief."

7. The reference is to Jesus's Parable of the Lost Sheep (Luke 15:3–7). There are three "lost" stories, of which this is one. The others are the woman searching for a lost coin (Luke 15:8–10) and the lost son (Luke 15:11–32) who comes to himself. Thurman is perhaps making an allusion to the latter in his reference to Jesus above. When the son "comes to himself (v. 17), he returns to his father who has been longing for him, the source from which he is alienated. See "Salvation: What Is God Like?" [1951] and "The Lost" [1957], in David B. Gowler and Kipton Jensen, eds., *Howard Thurman: Sermons on the Parables* (Maryknoll, NY: Orbis Books, 2018), 17–26; 78–87.

8. Francis Thompson (1859–1907) was an English Catholic poet and mystic. His poem "The Hound of Heaven" (1893) was a favorite poem of Thurman.

9. "The Over-Soul" (1841), in Ralph Waldo Emerson, *Essays and Lectures* (New York: Library of America, 1983), 383–400. Thurman, in "Plotinus: The Inward Journey," argues that Plotinus's influence on Emerson was "simply overwhelming," and mentions his impact on Wordsworth and Tennyson as well. For his influence on

ness the individual who experiences that begins to see that his soul, or that which is deepest in him, is the same as that which is deepest in the not-him, in somebody else. A sense of unity begins to emerge, which unity is disclosed to the individual out of his discovery that what is deepest in him is a clue to what is deepest in his neighbor.

But the soul isn't back yet according to Plotinus; it's on its journey. Now mark you, the soul is starting from where you and I are now, and we are moving up this way for the moment, figuratively, I mean. When the soul becomes aware of the over-soul, the world soul, which is the lung, the divine lung of the stuff of life, given that, now when it becomes aware of that through contemplation, through detachment, through withdrawal from sense involvements, the slavery to appetite, etc., it's the same, it's the same list all the time, wherever you touch it, it is the same list. Whatever may be the character of the religion, it is the same list. When the soul arrives through contemplation of the divine, it arrives to a point that it identifies itself with the divine thought; no differentiation between what it is and what it is thinking. But as long as there is awareness of thought there is self-consciousness, there is mind, which is, says Plotinus, the mind that we touch at the peak, the focal point of contemplation and meditation where the mind seems to envelop its object and become one with it. When that happens, we move into the knowledge that the ground of the soul, the ground of all of the expressions of life is mind, is intelligence. And as I, as the soul looks back over the way over which it has come, it knows without knowing and senses without being aware that every expression of life is an utterance of an intelligence and an order and a rationality. And then, says Plotinus, "When I arrive at a place," to use Kepler's phrase, jumping way ahead, "Oh, God I thank Thee that I think Thy thoughts after Thee. When I arrive at a place that I think God's thoughts after Him I still am not quite there."[10] Because where God is ultimately must be beyond thought and beyond intelligence, because all thought, all intelligence, has to do with differentiation; has to do with separateness; has to do with this as over against that. But when there is

---

Emerson, see Stanley Brodwin," Emerson's Version of Plotinus: The Flight to Beauty," *Journal of the History of Ideas* 35, no. 3 (1974): 465–83.

10. The German astronomer Johannes Kepler (1571–1630) is said to have said that "science is thinking the thoughts of God after him."

no thisness or thatness, no pro, no con, no tension, then all that we mean by thought disintegrates. So, Plotinus has his chute, and it is the point at which they all come, in one way or another. It is the final moment of complete ecstasy which seems so meaningless to those who live in this century and in this period of human history. And it seems meaningless to us because we are a generation that has been schooled in the dishonoring of our feelings. The only points at which we are permitted to honor our feelings are moments that are private, exclusively private and significantly intimate. Or moments that are completely outlawed like the alumni reunion, like the football game, like the race track. We do not honor our feelings; we are afraid of our feelings. And to be an intellectual, to be self-contained, to be an integrated human being is, according to the way we feel in modern life, is to be lopsided because nobody thinks his way through the world. You don't think your way through the world whatever you may think about what you think. No, you feel your way through the world. No man ever dies for an idea: he will die for an ideal because that has dynamics in it—energetics; it has a fringe of surging vitality in it. You don't find any reality to any syllogism however sound it is. That is what these men knew. So, they recognize the fact that there is a time when I move beyond all of the reflective processes of my mind, when all of the intellectual aspects of my personality break down under the overwhelming impact of that which is beyond the mind but envelops the mind. And everybody, at some moment in his life, in some tiny or dramatic aspect has been visited, always temporarily, by a surging something that sweeps him beyond the furthest rim of human thought, and then it turns him loose and he says, "Haaaah," and drops back into himself or herself.

Now, what Plotinus is saying, that the soul starts moving to make contact with the part of itself that it left behind and that movement is symbolic of the movement of the spirit of God in the life of man. And then on its way it becomes aware of itself, and becoming aware of itself, becomes aware of a world soul, an over-soul, which is in every one of us. And then on its journey, by further contemplation, by further meditation, by further prayer, it finally arrives at a point that it contemplates the divine thought, the divine idea, the divine reflection, the divine utterance: all these words they use. And then meditating upon that one arrives at a point that the thinker and the thought, the meditator and the meditation become one, one, but an awareness of this oneness is present. And then God, one comes into his presence finally without benefit of ascent of any ladders of logic but by what he calls the moment of the movement of the divine that creates the ecstasy in the heart. Therefore, to him there is a trinity: God, the unutterable who spills over into God the mind who becomes the ground of the soul and all other manifestations, and then God the soul whose unique revelation is in the human spirit.[11] And this was a man who loved little children and was so simple in his relationships.

---

11. In the *Enneads*, Plotinus identifies three principles, the One, the Intellect, and the Soul, which correspond to Thurman's use of "the trinity."

Saint Augustine

24 May 1953
Fellowship Church

For Thurman it was a paradox that "in the Christian religion, the greatest movement of mysticism has come out of the Roman Catholic Church."[1] For Thurman, the Catholic Church, with its rigid structures and dogmas, was the antithesis of the spiritual freedom mysticism required. Nowhere, perhaps, was this paradox for Thurman more heightened than with St. Augustine,[2] whose teachings form the bedrock of Roman Catholic orthodoxy, but whom he nonetheless viewed as "one of the great minds of the human race," and one of the great mystics, a man who had walked with God. In a 1950 sermon or unpublished lecture, "The Philosophy of History of St. Augustine,"[3] Thurman distinguished between two models of history, one that viewed history as circular,[4] and the other, St. Augustine's vision of history—and to a large extent Thurman's as well—"as an irreversible process moving in a definite direction." As a consequence, "history is a creative process. It grows into

---

1. "Men Who Have Walked with God: Lao-Tse," printed in this volume.

2. Saint Augustine of Hippo (original Latin name Aurelius Augustinus) was born 13 November 354, in Tagaste, Numidia (now Souk Ahras, Algeria), and died 28 August 430 in Hippo Regius [now Annaba, Algeria]. He served as bishop of Hippo from 396 to 430 and is considered by most scholars as the most influential Christian thinker after St. Paul. His written works, the most important of which are *The Confessions* (ca. 400) and *The City of God* (ca. 413–426), are classics in Western literature and shaped the theological and biblical foundations for much of medieval and modern Christian thought.

3. "The Philosophy of History of St. Augustine" (1950), in Folder 45, Box 7, HTC. This does not appear to be a Fellowship Church sermon. See also the two-part sermon, "The Inward Journey VII and VIII: St Augustine: Architect of a New Faith," 3 and 10 December 1961, in Folder 11, Box 14, HTC.

4. Thurman, in his lecture on Buddhism and Brahman mysticism in the "Men Who Have Walked with God," critiques circular and eternally recycling views of history.

organic unity with the growth of human experience. The past does not die; it becomes incorporated in humanity."[5]

In the sermon published here, Thurman suggests that in order to truly appreciate Augustine and his contribution to the church, one must gain a sense of his biography and the ways in which he struggled, as a young man, with his sexual desire, his belief in Manicheaism,[6] *and the need to transcend the limitations of its dualism. Thurman argues that buttressing Augustine's entire theology and philosophy is his mysticism. Although Augustine was, unlike Thurman, a "Christ mystic," he believed "there is in the human spirit . . . that which is not only like God, that which is not only an expression of God, but that which is God himself." Morality, therefore, Thurman adds, is the pragmatic outpouring of the mystical experience and "the method by which the God in man seeks to bring under subjection and control the total life of the individual. That in a word is the mystic's position."*

---

5. In *The City of God* (*De civitate Dei*) Augustine responds to the sack of Rome in 410 CE and makes the case for Christianity as being responsible for saving the city from total destruction. He further argues that there are two cities, the city of the elect and the city of the damned, and that human history can be interpreted through this lens. In "The Philosophy of History of St. Augustine," Thurman examines the philosophy of history as the means through which to best understand Augustine's view of the City of God. He contrasts two notions of time, one as circular and co-terminus with existence. In this view, says Thurman, there is no awareness beyond what occurs within cyclical dimensions of time. The other, writes Thurman, is linear and "suggests that within the time band the event may take on the character of the timeless, the finite may become involved in the infinite while it remains finite." It is this latter interpretation of time, says Thurman, that informs Augustine's interpretation of the two cities. "The earthly city, which aimed only at earthly prosperity, failed to attain even that, while the heavenly city, aiming at an eternal peace, supplies the best conditions for earthly goods as well."

6. Manichaeism was a religion that held a dualistic interpretation of good and evil. From its founding by Mani (216–274) in third-century Persia, its amalgam of Buddhism, Zoroastrianism, Christianity, and Gnosticism spread rapidly, and soon became a world religion, with adherents spread from North Africa to China. After several centuries of growth, Manichaeism declined, in large part because of persecution, though it lasted through the fourteenth century. Augustine was a lay believer in Manicheaism for nine years (373–382), but after his conversion, he became a fierce opponent and wrote several treatises denouncing the religion. For an overview, see Michel Tardieu, *Manichaeism* (Urbana: University of Illinois Press, 2008).

In 1961 Thurman offered additional perspectives on Augustine, speaking on the controversy between Augustine and the monk Pelagius,[7] who thought, contrary to Augustine, that human nature was basically good, which meant for Augustine that the individual did not need "any external socially dependent frame of reference in order [to] give redemptive character to the will." Thurman describes the dilemma of Augustine in confronting Pelagius, and was sympathetic to Augustine's position. "I want something that can protect me from self-deception. Something that will let me know by an other than self-reference when I am out of line. . . . I want to be safeguarded against being destroyed by the integrity of my own will. . . . I can't stand being solely dependent upon myself. And I can't stand not being dependent on myself."[8]

For Thurman, the questions Augustine faced amid the crumbling structures of the Roman Empire in the fifth century were the same questions that every person of religious faith still has to face. In 1961, with the civil rights movement no doubt on Thurman's mind and that of his listeners in Marsh Chapel, he had the following to say:[9]

> *Do you believe that there is the ground and the experience of your religion that which is so utterly significant in its transcendence and imminence and redemptive character as demonstrated in your life that it can provide a point of referral on the horizon that will be redemptive for our society, even to America, a basis for integrated behavior so that in the light of it, America can experience the kind of redemption that will make it whole. . . . Or is your personal experience of religion [so] small that you would not run the risk of giving it such a far-reaching assignment? This is the question with which Augustine wrestled.*

---

7. Pelagius (ca. 360–418 CE) was a Briton, probably of Welsh or Irish background, who lived in Rome and Carthage. He wrote extensively on free will and grace. His writings have been lost, and his theology is known primarily through the attacks of his opponents, such as Augustine.

8. "The Inward Journey VIII."

9. "The Inward Journey VII."

46 The Way of the Mystics

[Let us continue the "Men Who Have Walked with God" series][10] by considering one of the great minds of the human race. I refer to St. Augustine, the bishop of Hippo. I'm always impressed with the fact that it is a tribute to St. Augustine's greatness that almost anybody feels that he can take a potshot at him. I attended one of the discussions of the Great Books,[11] and I do not speak disparagingly, please, I say to myself, and I was interested in the fact that by the reading of a synopsis of *The Confessions* that the people who had this particular session had so many things to say about this man; and I could not keep from saying to myself what would they say about him if they had read the entire *Confessions*? I don't know, but it is a tribute to his greatness—not that there aren't many things about him that have given Western civilization a great deal of trouble.

I'd like to think carefully with you for a few minutes about him because he is the father of Roman Catholic mysticism.[12] And in many ways he represents one of those amazingly unique beings in human history: a man whose mind and whose grasp of the age in which he lived was so tremendous that he held in his hands the crumbling outposts of the Roman Empire until those disintegrating aspects of the empire could rally around a new point of integration and make it possible for the genius of the Roman Empire to be followed into the future; and thereby providing a light that has continued to illumine the darkness even down to latest time. There is so much that is fascinating about him that it requires a great deal of strength and control merely to lift out that which is relevant to our purposes this morning.

---

10. Hypothetical construction of missing opening sentence.
11. The Great Books of the Western World was a 54-volume set of extended excerpts from great philosophers, thinkers, and writers, released with great fanfare by the Encyclopedia Britannica in 1952. The Great Books project sponsored discussion groups in many cities to promote the series.
12. See Peter Brown, *Augustine of Hippo: A Biography* (rev. ed.; Berkeley: University of California Press, 2000). For a critical study of Augustine's mysticism, see John Peter Kenney, *The Mysticism of Saint Augustine: Rereading the Confessions* (New York: Routledge, 2005).

He was born in the fourth century. His father[13] was a so-called pagan, and his mother[14] was a devout, gentle daughter of the church. She was pious, spent much of her time in prayer both for her husband and for her son. The father focused all of his hopes on his son, which is a perfectly natural thing. He wanted his son to be a leader of a certain kind of thought. He gave him the best training possible, and his son grew up as a teacher, a professor of rhetoric. He taught rhetoric in his native city, but he found there that things were not—well, he was unhappy. He was unhappy not only because of things that were going on in his soul, but he was unhappy because his livelihood depended upon the students paying tuition and the students paid the tuition directly to the teacher. But these fellows at this university, I assume that they were fellows, would attend class right up to three days before the end of the term and then decide to change professors. So that Augustine found that over and over again life wasn't kind to him. He decided that he would go to Rome—go to Italy rather, and he went to Milan. There students were a little better, only they were rough and [as] well—students have been students a long time, haven't they?

When he went to Milan he came under the influence of a man who was a great preacher, Ambrose.[15] His mother did not want him to go to Milan because if she were unable to bring his wild and dynamic spirit under the gentle tutelage of the church when she lived with him in the same house and the same community, what chance would she have if he went to Milan—to Italy, that place far away from her restraining influence. So, the night before he left, she prayed all night asking God, "Please, don't let my boy take the boat." But even as she prayed, the boat pulled out and carried Augustine to Italy. And as it turned out that was the best

---

13. Patricius, one of the *curiales* of the city. In ancient Rome, a *curiales* was a leading member of a clan (*gentes*).

14. Saint Monica (322–387), Augustine's mother, is remembered as a woman of prayer and virtue; and it was her virtuous life and Christian faith, according to Augustine, that was responsible for his conversion.

15. Saint Ambrose (339–397), bishop of Milan, is remembered for both converting and baptizing Augustine and is credited with being his mentor. A highly literate and able preacher, Ambrose was also a skilled diplomat and apologist for the church. His theological perspective was deeply indebted to Philo, Origen, St. Basil of Caesarea, and the Neoplatonism of Plotinus, which also influenced Augustine.

thing that could have happened for him. It reminds me of a phrase that Havelock Ellis uses somewhere in his reflections, that after he became sixty years old he spent much of his time thanking God that God did not answer the prayers of his youth.[16] You see, this would be a terrible world if the only clues to the meeting of the deepest needs of the human spirit were in the hands of the people who had the needs: it would be a terrible world. And I am very glad that beyond my strength there is a greater strength, beyond my mind there is a greater mind, beyond my spirit a greater spirit or else there would be no way by which the errors of my mind and the blindness of my spirit could be absorbed, and I therefore can be protected and saved from myself. But anyway, Augustine went to hear Ambrose preach because he was interested not in what Ambrose was saying, but because he was interested in Ambrose's oratory, in his rhetoric. Ambrose was a spell-binder. But underneath all the magic of his words there was something else. And Augustine found that Ambrose's mind held him in tow while Ambrose's spirit took his spirit captive. And then certain questions began to stir in his mind. When Augustine came to Italy, he was a Manichean. Now don't let your minds stumble around over that. He was a Manichean, and Manicheans—we don't know quite what the origin of the cult or the sect was but basically the tradition is that they came from Persia, somewhere. But at any rate, their philosophy was very influential on Augustine's life. They believed that all of life is divided into a struggle between light and darkness. We have talked about that several times from the pulpit. Light and darkness, and the interesting thing is that these two powers, the powers of darkness and the powers of light, the God of darkness and the God of light, were not only two separate gods, two separate powers, but they were two powers that were equally matched. And it meant then that, for all eternity, the contradictions of human experience were ultimate and final contradictions; that there could be no way by which good could ultimately triumph, no way by which ultimately evil could triumph; and since the destiny was a tie

---

16. Speaking of a former romantic partner with whom he once contemplated marriage: "I have often felt thankful since that our prayers are not answered"; Phyllis Grosskurth, *Havelock Ellis: A Biography* (New York: Knopf, 1980), 17. Havelock Ellis (1859–1939) was a prolific English writer, best known as a pioneer sex researcher.

then how an individual lives was not particularly important because ultimately it made no difference in the way that things were balanced.

There was another force in Augustine's life, [and] that was the force of what must have been a very remarkable woman. When he was a young man his father, in order to protect him in some other ways, developed or was instrumental in developing an alliance between Augustine and a lady[17] who became the mother of his only child, all of this antedating his thirty-third year when he finally took his confession and became a Roman Catholic. And he loved this woman. They were never married. And when I talk about this, I do not mean to seem to be a peddler of unclean linen or to put the judgment of this age and this period upon his life; but it's important because of the bearing that it has on what flowered in his mind. And the thing that flowered in his mind has become so definitive in its effect on Western culture [and] Western civilization and that is why I want to say just a word about it. When he met Ambrose and came under the sweeping judgment of the mind and the spirit and the morality of this devoted and inspired Catholic priest, his very proximity to Ambrose began to raise in Augustine's mind certain searching questions about Augustine's own life. And one of the things that he had to face was what shall I do with this lady. And he and Ambrose struggled together, and then Augustine and the spirit of God struggled and Augustine and the spirit of Monica, his mother, struggled, and Augustine and the spirit of the age struggled. And so he would send her away and then bring her back, send her away, bring her back until at last out of the depths of his soul's conflict he discovered that only his total surrender to what to him at that time was the sovereignty of God would be able to resolve the inner conflict of his spirit, and he sent her away for good and turned his back upon all relationships that had to do with any dimension of the fulfillment of the flesh except the consumption of food. But the scar remained, and Augustine limps through the pages of human history bearing in his mind and in his body the agonizing struggle of the flesh with the spirit. And his struggle over this problem became the basis of his interpretation of the meaning of human depravity, the meaning of original sin. Original sin then becomes the sin of the flesh, and there is no way

---

17. Augustine never provided the name of his mistress in *The Confessions* or elsewhere. They bore a son, Adeodatus, who was baptized with Augustine by Ambrose.

by which man can be redeemed from the sin of the flesh, says Augustine, except by a definitive and radical act of God that picks the man up, purges him, and places him yonder. So that becomes the muted motif moving like a fleeting ghost through all of the massive revolvings of the mind of this tremendous man. God is sovereign, God is ruler, God is all that there is; and in the presence of God, mere man is but a pile of filthy rags. So deep and searching is the conflict in the soul of man that only a God who is the Creator of life and the soul is capable of redeeming man. That was what he felt and that moves into the heart of his great contribution, *The City of God,* [which] he was writing while the city of this world about which he had been writing was being destroyed. Think of it. Think of it for a moment. It is overwhelming. The barbarians pushing against every frontier; the Roman Empire had disintegrated and disintegrated and disintegrated through the radial expansion of slavery and conquest and with a corresponding loss of a sense of responsibility for the fate of the empire on the part of the average citizen; fear everywhere; men had lost their nerves. The eternal city was proving itself to be a time-born, time-eroded carcass. Is there any force anywhere capable of providing solidity and stability for this crumbling mass that at one time was the Roman Empire? No king can do it because the kings are interested in selfish plunder; no politician can do it; no mere philosopher can do it. The need is so vast, so tremendous that only someone who stands outside of human history and operates upon human history is capable of saving it. So in *The City of God* this is what Augustine works out, and it is that concept which subsequently the Roman Catholic Church began working on, you see, for a thousand years after Augustine's death; in which you gather up most of the creative aspects of the Roman Empire and you see them now redefining themselves in this hierarchical church. It is very interesting, but I won't go down that way.[18]

What Augustine felt in himself, you see, this collapse, this struggle he saw all around him in the empire. And just as only God could redeem him, Augustine, only God could redeem the empire. You see?

---

18. Thurman is referring to what theologians call "the Constantinian shift" or "Constantinian captivity of the church," the result of Emperor Constantine's conversion to Christianity and the eventual integration of the church into the hierarchical polity of the Roman Empire during the fourth century CE.

Saint Augustine 51

Now if God is the redeemer and only God, the sovereign whose will must be not only authentic but mandatory, then the vehicle through which this God expresses himself in time and space becomes *the* vehicle without which man cannot be pleasing to God. So, you get the doctrine, which is still the doctrine in the Roman Catholic Church that outside of this structure there can be no salvation.[19] And you see the logic that swings out of it from Augustine's mind and Augustine's dilemma.

Now if the church is the custodian of salvation as the representative, the earthly representative of the only sovereign God, then if I want to relate myself to the sovereign God, I must relate myself through this instrumentality, and this instrumentality expresses itself through the sacraments. And therefore, without these it is very difficult, if at all possible, to be pleasing to God. Now that's Augustine the theologian, Augustine the architect.

Now I will do the difficult thing. I will say just a few words about the Augustine in whom I am interested. I am interested in Augustine the man who gave to the world in his experience an interpretation of the meaning of mystical religion. May I refresh your minds that we began by saying that the basic insight of the mystic is that God is the Creator of all of life, including all living things, including all human beings. That there is in the human spirit, therefore, that which is not only like God, that which is not only an expression of God, but that which is God himself, and that the God in man which is the deepest thing in man, says the mystic, or the highest, constantly reaches out into life to make contact with the deepest thing in life knowing that what it finds out there, there being anywhere, is what it has already experienced in here. And that morality, as a derivative from that kind of religious experience is the method by which the God in man seeks to bring under subjection and control the total life of the individual: that in a word is the mystic's position.

Now, we saw how it was approached by these various people. Now just a word about Augustine in this particular, Augustine following Plato. He

---

19. The doctrine *extra ecclesiam nulla salus* (no salvation outside the church) was affirmed by many early church fathers, including Augustine, but did not become an official church dogma until the Fourth Lateran Council in 1215. The dogma was qualified but reaffirmed in the Second Ecumenical Council and subsequent papal encyclicals.

was profoundly influenced by Plato, more by Plato than by Aristotle, and so were the Greek fathers for that matter, the early church fathers. That's why some people feel that if you took Plato and Aristotle completely out of the Christian tradition and theology what we'd have left we would not be able to recognize. That's an overstatement of something that has a lot of truth in it. So, Augustine was deeply under the influence of Plato. At one point we see it expressed in his mysticism. Augustine felt that behind every, every manifestation was the real. That the real was not the "for instanced." And he has a beautiful passage somewhere in *The Confessions*, "I went to the skies and I asked the skies, "Are you He?" and the skies said, "No." I went to the wind and the breezes and they said, "No." I went to the denizens of the sea and the air and they said, "No." I went to my senses: taste, touch, smell. I said, "Are you He?" "No." Then I went to my soul. And my soul when I asked the question said, "That which is, is in me."[20]

Now, Augustine's mysticism follows the pattern of all of the rest of it, that there is what he calls at the top of the soul—you will notice the same phrase when we come to Eckhart[21] some weeks from now—at the top of the soul there is God, God. And that this is given, this is created, this is a part of the expression of human life, and that the will, the mind, are all vehicular of this. Now, he said that God in the mystic's journey [is] this mystic experience by which the illumination comes. Augustine goes through the senses; then he goes through the mind and exhausts reason and thought; he exhausts feelings and then he comes by the negative path[22] to that which is. That's the way he phrases it: that which is as over

---

20. Thurman is probably paraphrasing Augustine's *Confessions* 10.6.9: "And what is this? I asked the earth; and it answered, I am not He; and whatsoever are therein made the same confession. I asked the sea and the deeps, and the creeping things that lived, and they replied, We are not your *God*, seek higher than we. I asked the breezy air, and the universal air with its inhabitants answered, Anaximenes was deceived, I am not God. I asked the heavens, the sun, moon, and stars: Neither, say they, are we the God whom you seek? And I answered unto all these things which stand about the door of my flesh, You have told me concerning my *God*, that you are not He; tell me something about Him. And with a loud voice they exclaimed, *He made us.*"

21. Meister Eckhart, German theologian and mystic (ca. 1260–1328); see "Men Who Have Walked with God: Meister Eckhart," published in the current volume.

22. *Via negativa,* or in Christian mystical traditions, the way of describing what God or ultimate reality is by stating what God is not, which suggests that all finite descriptions of God are inadequate to ascertain the divine nature.

against that which is not. And then when he gets there he is beyond reflective analysis, beyond discursive thought, beyond articulate, broken-down feelings, spelled-out feelings. And he experiences union, says Augustine, union with Christ—he is a Christ mystic—union with God, which I experience without awareness of experiencing.

Now, the effect on Augustine was he used his mysticism, his mystical experience, as energy, as a source of energy and dynamics for sustaining him in these great undertakings of state and dogma to which he gave the resources of his mind. And I am impressed with him because usually we think of the mystic as someone who has taken his retreat from the world. But Augustine is one of the first great mystics in the Christian tradition, individualist though he is. He is not a group mystic; he isn't interested in any sort of fellowship in which all the people in the fellowship share this. He is a straight perpendicular mystic—no lateral in him. Nevertheless, there is a pragmatic result that comes from his experiences of union with God, and, as he would say, union through Christ as over against what Plato would say or Plotinus. But they are all talking about the same thing. There is a secondary utility that comes from this experience, and he doesn't seek union in order that he might get strength to do a job, but he seeks union because of the hunger in him that only God can answer. Once that hunger is met there is automatically released in him energy with which he does the hard job, the impossible job, bears the heaviest burden and suffers the greatest travail and misery. Therefore, we can all say with him, perhaps, those classic words that will be a part of the utterance of the human spirit as long as men are aware of the consciousness of God, "Behold, Thou hast made us for Thyself and our souls are restless 'til they find their rest in Thee."[23] And to that word of Augustine, the whole human race says, "Amen."

---

23. "You move us to delight in praising You; for You have made us for Yourself, and our hearts are restless until they rest in You [cor nostrum *inquietum* est donec *requiescat* in Te]" (Augustine, *Confessions* 1.1).

MAHATMA GANDHI

7 June 1953
Fellowship Church

Probably the best-remembered episode of Thurman's life was his meeting with Mahatma Gandhi on 21 February 1936.[1] He spoke and wrote about it often, and it has been often written about.[2] Gandhi and Rufus Jones were the only persons covered in the two "Men Who Have Walked with God" series whom Thurman had met, and in this sermon, as he often did when speaking about Gandhi, he included some anecdotes about their meeting. This sermon focuses on Gandhi's mysticism, and its connection to his social and political activism. For Thurman, Gandhi was one of the best exemplars of Eastern mysticism, seeking purification not for himself or his own soul but for humanity in general. If, for Thurman, Gandhi was, unquestionably, an "affirmation mystic," a world-famous politician, he was equally famous or

---

1. Mohandas Karamchand "Mahatma" Gandhi (1869–1948) was born in Gujarat, in British India. He studied law in London from 1888 to 1890 and moved to South Africa in 1893, where he developed many of his ideas about nonviolent resistance, and led his first *satyagraha* campaigns for Indian rights. In 1914 he returned to India and soon became a leader in the Congress Party and the fight for Indian independence. His many struggles with the British authorities, and his distinctive, ascetic lifestyle, soon attracted worldwide attention. Six months after India attained independence, he was assassinated in New Delhi.

2. For a longer account of Thurman's journey to India and meeting with Gandhi, see PHWT 1:180–339, and Quinton Dixie and Peter Eisenstadt, *Visions of a Better World: Howard Thurman's Pilgrimage to India and the Origins of African American Nonviolence* (Boston: Beacon Press, 2011), 65–151. The main source for Gandhi's meeting with the Negro delegation is the account, "With Our Negro Guests," written by Mahadev Desai, Gandhi's longtime personal secretary, published in *Harijan*, Gandhi's weekly English-language magazine, in March 1936, reprinted in PHWT 1: 332–39. This is supplemented by Thurman's many accounts of the meeting, including "Mahatma Gandhi," PHWT 3: 255–62 (1 February 1948); "The Quest for Peace," PHWT 4: 2–9 (24 July 1949); and the current sermon. For Thurman's account in his autobiography, see WHAH 130–35.

notorious for his uncompromising devotion to his ascetic religious practices. Thurman had criticized certain "life-denying" aspects of Brahman mysticism. But Gandhi showed that "it is possible to achieve effective worldly ends by the use of methods, techniques that are themselves unworldly." Thurman relates that when asked why, if he was such a pious Hindu, he didn't lead a more reclusive life, detached from the hurly-burly of pressing worldly events, he said that "I carry my cell with me, working in human relations, in politics, trying to clean up life around me. That is my purgation; that is my hair shirt; that is my discipline." For Thurman, Gandhi was a solitary mystic who needed to work "in the midst of the traffic of life." This was Thurman's aspiration as well.

We began with certain of the Christian mystics beginning primarily with St. Augustine. But I want to reach back today and pick up one who is outside of the immediate Christian tradition. It was a part of my plan to do him, but two weeks ago it just didn't seem right. I want to deal with certain aspects of the mystical insight of Mahatma Gandhi. I have here something which is very precious to me, and this has nothing to do with Mr. Gandhi's mysticism, but I just want you to see it. This is a piece of cloth that Mr. Gandhi—that's made out of thread that Mr. Gandhi wove, and he gave it to me when we were in India in 1935, and I just thought you might like to see it.[3]

You may recall that when we were talking about the Brahmanic mystics and Gautama Buddha considerable emphasis was placed upon the significance of the doctrine of ahimsa as it bore upon the relation between the inner life and the outer life. It was pointed out at the time that ahimsa deals basically with the attitude of the individual towards himself. It has to do with the purification of the individual's life. It is, in its out-going manifestation, it is non-resistance, it is passive, it is non-active really; but not because of how the individual conceives of himself as being related to the other person, but rather because the attitude that is ahimsa, the quality of life that is ahimsa, is one which purifies the individual. The true doctrine, the true genius of ahimsa, would say, "I will

---

3. The piece of hand-spun woven cloth, which was sent to Thurman shortly after his return to the United States in April 1936, is now at Morehouse College in Atlanta.

not kill you, [not] because you are sacred or because you love your life; but it says I will not kill you because if I kill you I defame myself." Now, that's the essence of it laid bare, the very anatomy of the doctrine of not killing; which is related therefore, you see, to the whole mystical experience of purgation, of self-purification as a part of the discipline through which the individual passes from his attachment in life and in experience through detachment from life and experience to illumination and then union. That's the process.

We discovered how the Buddha gave a positive quality, a life-affirming quality to this life-denying doctrine of ahimsa by injecting into the relationships a quality of compassion and a certain quality of reverence. He lifted the metaphysical doctrine of reverence for life to a category that was ethical in character. So that I revere life, and because I revere life, I will be compassionate to all living things.

Now, that is the background of Mr. Gandhi. The story of his life is very well known to all of us I suppose. I need not take time to go into detail concerning it. There are two or three things, however, that I want to point out. I asked him, and you will pardon the—that part of it, but there is only one way to say that and that is the way I am saying it—I asked him, when at last we had a chance to see him, a chance that I thought we were going to miss because each time a date was set for us to get together he was sick. Two weeks before leaving India, in Bombay we were, early one morning I decided that I would have to do something about it. You know, you wait for life to move and then if life doesn't decide that it understands what you are talking about, then you try to give it some instructions. So I decided I would send him a telegram to find out whether we could go down to his place in Wardha to see him or do something because two weeks and we would be coming back to America, and to come back to America without having a chance to see him. So when I walked out of the house at which we were living I met a man at the gate who had on a Gandhi cap, and he looked at me and we passed each other and sort of spoke on the ground. I decided to speak and he decided to speak, and then we both decided we didn't know whether we should speak—it was that sort of moment, you know—but we finally got by each other and then he turned around and he said, "Are you, you?" And I said, "Yes," and then he said, "I have a letter from Gandhiji." And I said, "That is interesting, because I am going to the post office now to send him a telegram." So I read the letter. The letter said that he was down at the neighbor state in Bardoli[4] and on his way back up to his ashram. He was not very well, traveling with his doctor; and he wondered whether we could interrupt our schedule at the university and come down to this place in Bardoli to see him, and then his letter said an amazing thing. I'll never get over it if I live forever. He said, "If your schedule is so busy, so crowded that you cannot take time to come down here to see me, and if at the end of the schedule you must get your boat so there is no time there to come to see me, I will get on the train with my doctor and come to Bombay to see you."[5] Think of it. The great Mahatma Gandhi. I tell you I'll never get over it. Well, of course, you can imagine what happened. We just cancelled the rest of everything and went down there. Three hours we spent talking by the watch, and he had the watch, a big silver watch that he put out in front of him. He said, "We have only three hours, and there are many things that I want to know, and we want to talk about and let's do it by the clock, by the watch." At the end I wanted to know one or two things, and Mrs. Thurman wanted to know one or two things, and he agreed to answer us because all the time we had spent answering his questions about America, and about American Negroes and about Africans and so forth. I wanted to know from him why did his doctrine of ahimsa with the things that he added to it, non-cooperation, etc., why did that fail of its objective, namely, to bring to the Indian people freedom. And he said to me that the doctrine failed because, number one, it was a creative ethical doctrine with a spiritual foundation. Now follow his thinking, now—with a spiritual foundation, and it would be effective only in the life that was so disciplined, so disciplined that it, the life, could handle this ethical doctrine with its spiritual foundation. And he said, "The masses of Indians can't do that, because," said he, "they are lacking in vitality. And they are lacking in vitality for two reasons. The first reason is they are hungry." And then he talked statistics about the number of Indians who live and die, etc., without getting enough food to eat and on and on and on. And

---

4. Bardoli was one of the over five hundred states in British India. It had a somewhat greater degree of self-governance than areas under direct British control.

5. The letter is not extant, and Thurman never told this story of Gandhi's willingness to come to Bombay with his doctor to meet the Negro delegation.

he said, "I had to withdraw from politics, from active politics and go into something else. I had to do something about this poverty. And during the long months, six months during which the season is dry and farming is impossible, the villagers are idle and they starve. Now if we could recapture the lost cottage industry by reintroducing the cottage spinning wheel, then we could make a fundamental attack on this question of poverty." So the spinning wheel became the symbol, the vehicle by which this man sought to attack the problem not of poverty as such but to make it possible for the average Indian to deal creatively with the doctrine of ahimsa. That is the thing to remember. Don't forget that. Incidentally, of course, it meant an attack on poverty, and etc.

Then, the second reason for their lack of self-respect was the presence of untouchability in Hinduism.[6] And I expected him to say that they had lost their self-respect because of the presence of the conqueror in their midst. That [the British] were there and had been there for two or three hundred years and had done this and this and this and this. No, he said none of that. But we have lost our self-respect because we practice, as Hindus, we practice untouchability. Tremendous! So he began working at it. The first thing he did as a caste Hindu was to adopt into his family, as a member of his family, a girl who was untouchable. And at the time he did that, the plight of the untouchable was so terrible in South India that an untouchable was not even permitted to cross a street on which was located a Hindu temple because his shadow would contaminate it. At that moment, this man adopted, as a member of his family, one of these people. And he said to all of the caste Hindus, "This is what I mean by what I am saying." And then a second thing he did was to change the name from untouchable or *Shudras* or *Haris*, depending upon the part of the country, to *Harijans*.[7] And the word *Harijan* means child of God.

---

6. If Gandhi opposed untouchability, he did not oppose the caste system as such, and Thurman was, if reluctant, somewhat sympathetic (or at least not dismissive) of Gandhi's position. Thurman wrote in 1938: "I do not know enough about India whether caste is good or bad for that land. On the surface of it, it seems to me very bad in many ways. But this is a superficial and uncritical judgment. I think untouchability is a very terrible thing because it destroys every vestige of self-respect on the part of the outcast" ("India Report," PHWT 2: 136–37).

7. Gandhi began his campaign against untouchability in 1932, and renamed his weekly journal *Harijan* the following year. The term was considered patronizing by

And he said, with a wonderful cherubic chuckle, he said, "I felt that if I could make every caste Hindu call an outcaste, every time he referred to him, a child of God, I would in that act create for the caste Hindu the kind of moral problem that could never be solved until he changed his attitude towards the untouchable. Tremendous, isn't it? Let that soak in. It's tremendous. So his magazine changed the name of his publication to *Harijan*.

Now what is back of all of this? Here is a man, and this is how it relates to our series. Here is a man who is rooted in the basic, the basic mysticism of the Brahman, who inherits as one of the ethical overtones of his Hindu path the application of the doctrine of ahimsa to individuals and to relationships with individuals that extend beyond that of merely self-purification; which says, you see, that it is possible to achieve effective worldly ends—mark all the words, please—that it is possible to achieve effective worldly ends by the use of methods, techniques, that are themselves unworldly. Now, think about it. Don't hurry over it even though the time is getting away. Just think about it, that it is possible to achieve worldly ends—the thisness ends, pro-ing and con-ing ends, conflicts, the contradictions of experience, all of the tensions by which the individual's life is twisted because the good that he sees he is unable to achieve, and the good that he sees again and again he does not want to achieve—that it is possible, it is possible to deal with the materials that are inherent in the traffic of life, to deal with them effectively and creatively by the use of means and methods that are themselves derived from another kind of orientation. Now that's what he is saying.

So, ahimsa then becomes a doctrine of ethics which is life affirming, even though in genius the doctrine is life denying; for it says, you see, as Gandhi very adequately expressed it, that whatever may be the matter of the time-space involvement of the human spirit, they are always rooted in a dimension of life that transcends time and space; that there is no such thing as an activity that is not rooted and grounded in a realm that transcends that activity. That is what he is saying. And if it be true, then,

---

many untouchables, and Dalit is now the preferred designation. Shudras are the lowest level (save the outcastes) in the traditional Indian caste system. Hari is a Muslim term for Dalits.

that there is a quality that is spiritual that undergirds the total operation of life's adventure, then he who is able to deal with things on the surface of life, from within the knowledge that he has of the depths of life, will be able to gather in the total sweep of his living, a creative synthesis in which there is at least no conflict and no frustration. That is what he is saying. Do you believe that? You believe that? I wonder. We believe it in little ways, don't we? We believe it in little ways. If you have a problem in your own life, and this merely has to do with your digestion, you know; for some reason it isn't operating properly and you think about various things. You say, well, something disagreed with me, or I should have known better than to have eaten a cucumber at twelve o'clock at night, or something like that. But if it keeps happening you keep fooling with it. You begin to dig back behind that, don't you? Maybe I am worrying too much; maybe I'm getting too tired; maybe I am. . . . And you go on. And little by little by little by little you push, push, push, push back until at last that which is movement on the surface of your life is but manifestation of stirrings at the depth of your life. That is what he is talking about.

Now let's see the kind of thing that it made me do (and I'll be through in two or three minutes, I hope). When one of his ascetic friends chided him because he was becoming involved more and more in thisness and thatness, more involved in conflict, in life, instead of withdrawing into the foothills or some other place in the Himalayas and there practicing his purgation—and there is something to be said for that. We have talked about it once before; this deep insistence that keeps turning up in the human spirit, that somehow I must, at long last, withdraw. And in my withdrawing I am able to bring to bear upon the total problems of existence a total self that isn't scattered in this and that and the other, and perhaps if I can do that, and men always rise up in our society who feel this way and who are under great conviction and who have a tremendous contribution to make to our disorder. If they can sufficiently purgate themselves and at last get the illumination and be bathed in the light of His presence so that there is no longer any awareness of darkness and I do not know which is I and which is He, there are men who feel that if that can happen then the world can be redeemed, and only that way. So, when such a man wrote to Mahatma Gandhi chiding him because he was trying to clean up the world—clean up India and doing a lot of other things, "Why don't you withdraw to your cell?" And Gandhi said, "I carry my cell with me, working in human relations, in politics, trying to clean up life around me. That is my purgation; that is my hair shirt; that is my discipline. I do not offer it to you," he said, "but for me, working in the traffic is the discipline. And if I, in the midst of the traffic of life, can walk with the independence of solitude, as Emerson said, then every struggling man caught by the agonizing pressures of his life from which there seems to be no relief can take hope.[8] Because where he is in his trap, surrounded by the intimacy of his own agonies, there he can see God's face and be transformed. And that's why the masses of the Indian people found in this strange little man the door to all their hopes. And it is easier to believe both in the love and the wisdom of God because he left so great a witness in so humble a man.

---

8. "It is easy in the world to live after the world's opinion; it is easy in solitude to live after our own; but the great man is he who in the midst of the crowd keeps with perfect sweetness the independence of solitude"; Ralph Waldo Emerson, "Self-Reliance" (1841), in Emerson, *Essays and Lectures*, 263.

Saint Francis

14 June 1953
Fellowship Church

There was no more popular saint in twentieth-century America, especially among non-Catholics, than St. Francis of Assisi; and he was especially beloved by pacifists, environmentalists, and those, like Thurman, attracted to unconventional and non-institutional expressions of spirituality.[1] Thurman had long admired St. Francis.[2] In this sermon, Thurman briefly retells the life journey of St. Francis of Assisi (1181–1226). Born into a wealthy family in Assisi, in the duchy of Spoleto, he early lived a life of luxury. He was captured in war, and while in captivity he began receiving visions that led him to devote his life in service to the poor. Thurman rehearses the well-known stories of his encounter with the leper; his vision before an old Byzantine crucifix at the church of San Damiano where God told him, "Go repair my church, which as you see is falling completely in ruin"; and the story of his vision in 1224 that left him with the stigmata of Christ.

As in other sermons in this series, Thurman focuses on the themes of detachment and compassion for all creatures as both spiritual and moral priorities: "that there is active and actively at work in him the very vital awareness of the love of God, which love is harmonious, is integrating, is whole.

---

1. See Patricia Appelbaum, *St. Francis of America: How a Thirteenth-Century Friar Became America's Most Popular Saint* (Chapel Hill: University of North Carolina Press, 2015).

2. Thurman wrote, while studying with Rufus Jones, what he called in his autobiography "a definitive study of the mysticism of St. Francis of Assisi" (WHAH 77), which, alas, is no longer extant. In November 1943, the Lincoln Players (from Lincoln University) presented: "A Disciple of St. Francis" at Rankin Chapel under Thurman's supervision, providing an opportunity, he wrote, that "deepened our sense of appreciation for the life of one of the great exponents of Christianity who sprang from the loins of the Roman Catholic Church" (PHWT 3: 75).

To continue our series about Men Who Have Walked with God [with a sermon on] St. Francis of Assisi. I want to read something. He didn't write it, but it's about him and it catches his spirit. Just a part of it, I won't take the time to read it all. "St. Francis to the Birds":[3]

> Little sisters, the birds:
>   We must praise God, you and I—
>   You, with song that fills the sky,
> I with halting words
> . . . .
> Little flowers of air,
>   With your feathers soft and sleek,
>   And your bright brown eyes and meek,
> He hath made you fair.
> He hath taught to you
>   Skill to weave, in tree and thatch,
>   Nests where happy mothers hatch
> Speckled eggs of blue
> And hath children given,
>   When the soft heads overbrim
>   The brown nests, then thank ye Him
> In the clouds of heaven.
> Also in your lives
>   Live His laws, Who loveth you.
>   Husbands, be ye kind and true
> Be home keeping wives
> Love not gossiping;
>   Stay at home and keep the nest;
>   Fly not here and there in quest
> Of the newest thing.

---

3. Kathleen Tynan, "St. Francis to the Birds," in *The Poems of Kathleen Tynan* (ed. Monk Gibbon; Dublin: Allen Figgis, 1963), 60–62. Kathleen Tynan (1861–1931) was an Irish poet and a prominent figure in the Irish literary revival.

[Talking to the birds, of course.[4]]
Live as brethren live:
    Love be in each heart and mouth.
    Be not envious, be not wroth,
Be not slow to give.
    When ye build the nest
    Quarrel not o'er straw or wool.
He, He hath be bountiful to the neediest.
Be not puffed nor vain
    Of your beauty or your worth,
    Of your children or your birth,
Or the praise you gain.
Eat not greedily.
Sometimes for sweet mercy's sake"
[this is lovely][5]
Worm or insect spare to take;
Let it crawl or fly.
See ye sing not near
    To our church on holy day
    Lest the human-folk should stray
From their prayers to hear.
    Now depart in peace:
    In God's name I bless each one;
May your day's be long i' the sun
And your joys increase
And remember me,
    Your poor brother Francis, who
    Loves you, and gives thanks to you
For this courtesy
Sometimes when ye sing
    Name my name that He may take
    Pity for the dear song's sake
On my shortcomings.

---

4. Thurman's interjection, probably expressing his embarrassment at the patriarchal implications of Tynan's poem.

5. Another interjection.

There is something about life, for lack of a better characterization, that says that life is alive; that life is dynamic and that there are purposes and ends, goals that extend beyond the little purpose and the little goal and the little end of the little or the big man. In other words, life seems to me to be working towards fulfillment in the large and gross, in the sense that they are unrefined as far as the particular mind is concerned, but in the sweep of the life process, ends are achieved that are greater than any little ends. And perhaps, perhaps, perhaps if a man can be sufficiently sensitive, consciously or unconsciously, to relate his little purpose to the big purpose, his little goal to the big goal, his little end to the big end, then the strength and the power and the fullness of the big purpose and the big goal and the big end may give vitality to the little purpose and the little goal and the little end.

Now that sounds a long way from St. Francis, but it isn't really, because St. Francis came along at a time when the lights were going out everywhere. The church had become sterile, and the medicine of salvation of which the church at that time was the custodian, the dispenser, was giving only to those who rated it in one way or another, because they were able to pay or because they could pile up enough deeds, etc. The little man with his little hopes was desolate. And God moved in, in the heart of a little valley, and stirred a man who became the answer to the darkness. And life is always doing that, isn't it? Always doing that because life is its own restraint; because life is alive, and dynamic. Any study of history reveals many illustrations of this thing. Just to take one to which I have referred many times from this pulpit: in the early nineteenth century, 1805–1806, when Napoleon was at the height of his power, strutting across Europe like some mighty colossus, dominating the whole horizon so that all men who looked in any direction could not see the light because of his shadow. What happened? In England at least two babies were born right at the peak of Napoleonic power. One was Charles Darwin, and you can see what the work of Darwin's mind did to all the presuppositions that a Napoleon had. There was another, of course, Mendelssohn, but I am not intelligent enough to know how—too much about how that bears. But the other, a baby was born in a log cabin in Kentucky—and his name was Abraham Lincoln—precisely at the moment of what seemed to have been the greatest bankruptcy. It is interesting.[6] So we are not surprised that St. Francis comes along at a time when the lights are out. Life is like that, I think.

Francis came from a very wealthy family. You know his story well. I'll just give it in bold outline and then come at once to where he belongs in this procession. He lived gaily, a man of great joy, a troubadour first by the grace of self and then later by the grace of God, troubadour nevertheless. And then one day he stopped for prayer in a wayside chapel, a chapel that had fallen into disrepair, and the moment of turning into the chapel was the climax of a long inner process that had been at work in this man's sensitive spirit, a process that was bringing him closer and closer to the kind of decision that would transform his life. He knelt and he prayed, and when he opened his eyes the crucifix that needed restoration opened its eyes and said to him, "Repair my church." Now we need not waste any time on whether or not the crucifix spoke, on what Francis saw, because all the words that we use about it will be descriptive words. They will not have to do with the thing itself. It is sufficient to say that Francis, when he heard the voice, surrendered his life. And when he surrendered his life, so much energy that had been dammed up in him by his inner conflict was released that he became a new man. And we may explain it in any way we wish. The fact is he came into this place in one condition, and he came out in a new and radically different condition. It's like the figure that Carl Sandburg describes about the violinist, the man who went up in the gallery to hear Mischa Elman play the violin. He spent his last twenty-five cents; he was about to commit suicide; all life had caved in on him. But he said, "I'll spend this last quarter and go up and get a seat in the gallery," says Carl Sandburg about this man, "and hear Mischa Elman play the violin once before I die." And when Mischa Elman began playing the violin, the dam broke in the man who heard. And Carl Sandburg in his quaint and wonderful manner says, and "when he came downstairs out of the gallery his feet hit the sidewalk in a new way."[7] Now that is the thing.

---

6. Charles Darwin and Abraham Lincoln were born on the same day, 12 February 1809. The German-Jewish composer Felix Mendelssohn (1809–1847) had been born in Hamburg about a week earlier, on 3 February.

7. "When he got outside his heels hit the sidewalk in a new way. He was the same man in the same world as before. Only there was a singing fire and a climb of roses everlastingly over the world he looked on"; from "Bath," in Carl Sandburg, *Chicago*

Now what happened we won't try to talk about at the moment, but that it happened is crucial and important.

So Francis renounced a lot of things. He was a disappointment to his father because his father had ambitions for him, and when he came in with this idea about surrendering his life then that didn't make very much sense. So there was some legal matter that was referred to the bishop having to do with property rights, etc., and Francis, when the hearing was called, just bundled all of his clothes that he had, that he owned, put them under his arm and walked into the hearing without a stitch on and said well, "Here it is. That's the end of your claim on me." It's very dramatic and may not be true.[8] But the important thing is that they said he did it, and that indicates the measure of impact of the man's mind on his contemporaries. That is the important thing.

Then he began making certain discoveries, and I want to talk about these because it is in this area that his mysticism looms large. He is an uncomplicated mystic. He isn't bothered about trying to understand the Godhead and the soul and how the Godhead manifests itself, as we will be seeing when we talk about Eckhart.[9] He isn't interested in any of the metaphysical problems, any of the theological problems or the philosophical problems. The only thing he knows is that there is in his heart a song, which song is an expression of the love of God as the love of God manifests itself in Francis. And it is this same music that he hears when he listens to another person's heart. It is the same music that he hears when he looks at the birds or the sun or the flowers.[10] The love of God singing in

---

Poems (New York: Henry Holt, 1916), 56. Mischa Elman (1891–1967), a Ukrainian-born, Jewish-American violinist, was one of the most prominent classical musicians of his time.

   8. The popular narrative is that in 1206, his father, Pietro di Bernardone, a wealthy textile tradesman, disappointed and angry, took Francis before the bishop of Assisi, demanding repayment for his cloth and one of his horses that were sold and the money used to buy stones and materials for the rebuilding of the church. Francis strips before his father, returning his clothes and renouncing his inheritance.

   9. See HT, "Men Who Have Walked with God: Meister Eckhart," 5 July 1953, printed in this volume.

   10. As Thurman rightly describes, St. Francis wrote poetry and music for many images in nature.

his heart: and the love of God that is in every other living thing answers the music. That's all Francis says.

He gathered around him some followers.[11] When this creative thing which was in him began moving, it had to be organized, you know. Organization is very important. It is the way by which great creative concepts are kept from disintegrating, and also it is the way by which they are embalmed. In order to have the right of this order, the pope gave him permission, but the ultimate authority rested with the pope, etc. Francis had no interest in all of that, really. All he wanted to do was love people and be loved by them and respond to them naturally and simply without ambiguities. Near the end of his life he had the great experience. It was Easter, and he had been praying and meditating on the life of Jesus Christ, on the suffering; and he sought God to please permit him to experience in his body the suffering of Jesus Christ, and in his heart the love of Jesus Christ. Interesting combination. And as the sun rose on Easter morning, a great tidal wave of unrelenting emotion swept up through him and engulfed him, and identified all of his being with what he felt was the resurrected Christ standing in the shafts of light from the morning sun. When that happened to him, he looked at his hands, and in his hands and in his feet and in his side there was the stigmata; there was the blood. There were about forty-two (the last time I checked this was ten years ago) at that time; there were on record forty-two cases of the stig-

---

11. The Franciscans are a related group of Roman Catholic mendicant orders. In 1209, Pope Innocent III approved the creation of the Order of the Franciscans. The order began with Francis and eleven of his followers who became the first Franciscan friars with a simple rule: they could own no possessions of any kind, either individually or communally. Debates over the strictness of this rule led to splits among the Franciscans, which soon became one of the most powerful orders in the Catholic Church. The Spiritual Franciscans, or Fraticelli, strict followers of the ideas of St. Francis, clashed with the church hierarchy and were declared heretical in 1296. The Franciscans today consist of three orders: the First Order comprises priests and lay brothers who have sworn to lead a life of prayer, preaching, and penance; the Second Order consists of cloistered nuns who belong to the Order of St. Clare (O.S.C.) and are known as Poor Clares (P.C.); and the Third Order consists of religious and lay men and women who try to emulate St. Francis's spirit by performing works of teaching, charity, and social service. In 2013 Argentinian cardinal Jorge Mario Bergoglio chose Francis as his papal name.

mata: of men or women who experience at the moment of great critical identification, in their bodies the wounds of Jesus.[12]

One other thing about him, and then I pick up the thing that I want to pinpoint. He battled with disease all of his life. About twenty years ago a little book was written called *Fighters of Fate*.[13] It is the story of a group of men who had wrestled with tuberculosis and who had won the battle. And one of the most inspiring chapters in that little book is the chapter on St. Francis's struggle with tuberculosis and his triumph over it.

Now he died feeling that as far as the great order that bears his name is concerned, it would have been much better if he'd never been involved in it. But he also died feeling that in his life the love of God had been so operative that all who knew him in kind.

Now in a general way that's the story of Francis. There are two things about it to which I want to call your attention now. It's what he does about poverty, how his renunciation—bear in mind now what the basic proposition is—that there is active and actively at work in him the very vital awareness of the love of God, which love is harmonious, is integrating, is whole. And the degree to which the individual in all of the dimensions of his life and personality becomes completely involved in the love of God, to that degree will he relax his interest in preferences as he lives. Now that's very interesting. Now if you think about it very hard for a minute (I know it's warm in here and a little on the sleepy side) but think hard for just a minute. It is the bias of the personality for preferences that create so many of the complicated problems of living. For instance, when Francis relaxed his insistence upon preferences, one of the first things that manifested itself was his dealing with lepers. All of his life he had

---

12. The word "stigmata" (wounds of Christ) refers to five marks: two on his palms and two on his feet, where the nails that fixed Christ to the cross were traditionally believed to have been hammered, and the fifth on his side, left by a Roman centurion. According to one student of the subject, approximately four hundred persons, the majority of them women, have claimed to exhibit the stigmata, all since St. Francis; Ted Harrison, *Stigmata: A Medieval Mystery in a Modern Age* (New York: Penguin Books, 1999). Probably the most famous stigmatic since St. Francis is the Italian friar Padre Pio (1887–1968), canonized in 2002.

13. J. Arthur Myers, *Fighters of Fate: A Story of Men and Women Who Have Achieved Greatly* (Baltimore: Williams & Wilkins, 1927), 97–103. Thurman's first wife, Katie Kelley, died of tuberculosis in 1930.

had an instinctive revulsion against lepers. He would do anything to help anybody, but he simply could not abide having primary face-to-face contact relations with lepers. But he relaxed his insistence upon preferences, things that I enjoy to do, things that I do not enjoy to do. Then he bathed the leper, took care of them, lived there for a while without feeling that he was doing something merely for the good of the leper; not feeling that he was doing something for the good of his own soul, but all questions of appraisal with reference to the thing that is done are relaxed because, says Francis, in the love of God there can be no disharmony. So if I move into the living situation from within the spirit and the mood of the harmony which is the love of God, then I take into the disharmony that which works like a catalytic agent bringing peace out of chaos, tranquility out of confusion. Tremendous thing. I just look at him and long with all my heart that someday I will be able to do that.

Now the other thing. What he does, he takes the same principle, and applies it to poverty, which is another dimension of renunciation. His acceptance of poverty isn't because he wants to make sacrifices, and it doesn't have to do primarily or exclusively with money, with gold. But anything that creates in the mind attitudes of disharmony, of scatteredness, of divisiveness, of divided allegiances, divided loyalties has to be renounced, even the doing of good deeds if necessary. If I find that I am wedded to the doing of good deeds, then the center of focus becomes that, and the good deed is no longer vehicular of the loving spirit or the will of God. Even the church might become—and for Francis to feel this in the thirteenth century is something—might become that which is an end in itself. If it becomes an end in itself then it is no longer vehicular, then it has to be renounced: this is not thine. So he embraced poverty as an attitude towards life which made it possible in his spirit not to become attached to things, because the interesting thing about things is that when you get them they take over.

I am sure I have told you about this: when I was a senior in divinity school or middler, a friend of mine gave me a very beautiful, thin gold Elgin watch. And up to that time I'd only had an Ingersoll watch, you know, that made a loud noise. And I would put it on the pulpit when I was talking, and with a lot of silence in between you could hear the thing tick away; and this friend decided that he would do something about it, so he gave me this beautiful watch. Well I had for six months been conducting a study group two-and-a-half miles across town. This was in Rochester, New York, and we would begin at ten o'clock at night and go on until twelve, twelve-thirty and then I would walk home down Main Street, one o'clock, one-thirty.[14] But after I was given this watch, then I changed my route completely. I walked only where there were bright street lamps because I did not want anybody to take my watch. I didn't worry about what they would do to me, you see, so that I became involved in my identification with this thing.

Things are tyrannical; they squeeze, and there is no way by which we can disentangle ourselves unless we relax our attachment, not so much to the things but to what the things symbolize in our minds. That's the thing. It is my identification with status, my identification with security, my identification with this or the other that makes me take the symbol and hug it to my breast until it chokes me to death. Now Francis saw that and he said, "Don't do it!" Disciples or his followers, his troubadours, reminded him of a very interesting thing, that a rich man is also a child of God. Interesting! The obligation to seek the response, the movement of the love of God in my heart reaching to make music with the movement of the love of God in Christian's heart must not be obstructed by the category into which I place the other man. So he is a Communist; so I can't hear the music of the love of God; he's a Democrat, he's a Republican, he's Catholic, he's Buddhist, he's a Korean, he's a Baptist, he's rich, he's poor, he's ugly, he's beautiful, he doesn't wear decent clothes, he's overdressed, he has bad mannerisms, he's crude—all of these things, my friends, when they become the way by which we imprison another, then the music of the love of God in the heart can't make music with them. And he who builds obstructions that become divisive, walling off one man from another because of politics, creeds, predicaments, status, or class, is against God, whose will is that the love in my heart will make music with the love in your heart.

And I am grateful to Francis and to God both for the inspiration and the judgment that his life places over my own.

---

14. For Thurman's late-night class with Black women at the YWCA, most of whom worked as servants and maids, see "Men Who Have Walked with God: Lao-Tse," published in this volume.

Jane Steger

21 June 1953
Fellowship Church

"*I encountered her in 1925. . . . I was in a very bad state of mind. I'd gone through a circling series of impossible tragedy and a friend of mine sent me this copy. I'd never heard of her. And I read it and reread it and it's the one book that I never lend because I don't.*"[1] So Thurman spoke of Jane Steger's Leaves from a Secret Journal[2] *in a 1978 lecture. He had recently helped reprint Steger's book, originally published in 1926.*[3] *He had long been the most prominent of a small group of her ardent admirers.*

Of all the subjects in the Men Who Have Walked with God series Steger was by far the most obscure, the only woman, and was the only one still living. Jane Steger was a pen name of Margaret Prescott Montague (1879–1955), a popular author of novels and works of Southern folklore.[4] *She also had an abiding interest in Christian mysticism and had written previously a short book about an earlier mystical experience.*[5] *After discovering Steger's work,*

---

1. HT, "Mysticism and Social Change," #14, 27 July 1978, part of a course Thurman taught at the Pacific School of Religion. Since Steger's book was published in 1926, it seems unlikely this conversation took place in 1925.

2. Jane Steger, *Leaves from a Secret Journal: A Record of Intimate Experiences* (Boston: Little Brown, 1926).

3. Steger, *Leaves*.

4. Margaret Prescott Montague (1879–1955) spent most of her life in Virginia and West Virginia. Her works of local folklorist fiction include *The Sowing of Alderson Cree* (New York: Baker & Taylor, 1907), and *Home to Him's Muvver* (New York: E. P. Dutton, 1916). Her short story "England to America," published in the *Atlantic Monthly* in September 1918, won the initial O. Henry Prize for the best American short story of the year. It is reprinted in Finely M. K. Watson and Homer A. Watt, *Voices of Liberty* (New York: Macmillan, 1941), 577–92. Biographical information on Montague is scarce, but see Mary Newton Stannard, "Margaret Prescott Montague," *The Bookman* 52, no. 5 (January 1921): 317.

5. Margaret Prescott Montague, *Twenty Minutes of Reality: An Experience with Some Illuminating Letters Concerning It* (New York: E. P. Dutton, 1917). Her final

as he explains in the sermon, he knew he had discovered another kindred spirit, a Christian mystic uninterested in the outer forms of Christianity, a mystic who formed an intense bond with the aliveness of the natural world. If Steger was more overtly Christian (and less overtly feminist) than Olive Schreiner, another woman whose writings had a great impact on him, the two women had much in common for Thurman.[6] *Both gave accounts of the latent spiritual power of women, for so long dismissed and confined. "Here in this life," wrote Steger, "we are like Jack-in-the-box. Our spirit is squeezed into something that is too small for it, with the lid hooked down tight; but every now and again, through the pressure of some high emotion, the lid flies off, we shoot up to our full height, and gaze with delighted eyes on a lovely new world."*[7] *Steger, says Thurman, felt that humans were still in "the blind puppy phase," because, "we are using our minds as equivalent to the way the puppy uses his nose and we feel that everything that is anything can be grasped by our little minds; that if it doesn't make sense to the mind then it has no sense at all," just "sniffing all over the place with our little intellects. But she says that there will come a time when our eyes will open" and "many things that I cannot grasp with my mind disclose themselves."*[8]

I shall continue the series with Men Who Have Walked with God by jumping way ahead of ourselves with a person of this [century], a con-

---

book, *Closed Doors: Studies of Deaf and Blind Children* (New York: Houghton Mifflin, 1934), also drew on her interest in the spiritual consequences of physical limitations.

6. For Olive Schreiner (1855–1920), the South African feminist, pacifist, novelist, and social theorist, and her influence on Thurman, see HT, ed., *A Track to the Water's Edge: An Olive Schreiner Reader* (New York: Harper & Row, 1973).

7. Steger, *Leaves*, 67.

8. On the same day Thurman delivered this sermon on Jane Steger, he offered a despairing meditation, probably as the opening of the sermon, on Julius and Ethel Rosenberg, who had been executed two days earlier for espionage. It is an indication of Thurman's range that he could speak on two such disparate topics in a single sermon. The editors decided the Rosenberg meditation would fit better in the next volume of the collected sermon series, a volume covering Thurman speaking on democracy and other political topics. At the very end of the sermon, he obliquely returns to the execution of the Rosenbergs, quoting Tolstoy, as he does at the end of this sermon, on his revulsion at watching a public execution. "Tolstoy says, 'that a level in me, deeper than thought, deeper than logic, deeper than my culture, deeper than my religious conviction, I knew that this thing was wrong.' Now it happens to us."

temporary practically, an American, and a woman who has left her record in a single little book which in many ways is one of the most suggestive and thoroughly and simply illuminating volumes that I have ever read. This book is twenty-five years old, and the title of it is *Leaves from a Secret Journal*, by Jane Steger. One thing I wanted to tell you about St. Francis last Sunday and I didn't think of it until Wednesday, but may I just say it in passing. One of the most wonderful stories about him is that when he died and went to heaven, he was so holy that as he moved through the gates, he took the gates off their hinges so that anybody who wishes can walk in. I think that is a nice story.

I would like to begin our thinking together about this very remarkable and very simple mystical spirit by reading a few lines from one of her things: [9]

> I sit in the center of myself
> And weave busy thoughts,
> Like a black spider making her web.
> I am so intent on my own spinning
> I can see nothing but the whirling of my own mind.
> If I could stop a moment and be still,
> I might take note of the gleaming dewdrops
> God hangs all over the gossamer of thought,
> His tremendous periods;
> I might see also the tapestry of other spiders
> Lying in gauzy freshness
> Everywhere on the grass of imagination.
> If I could get straight away
> From the center of my own weaving
> And kneel down, I might, indeed, perceive God Himself,
> But the little shuttles of thought
> Fly so fast, so fast,
> I'm deafened by their whir,
> Entangled in my own web,
> And choke by the limitations of self.

---

9. Steger, *Leaves*, 8–9.

Beautiful, that is I think so. I do not know any details concerning this remarkable person except as revealed by references that she makes to her own situation in the pages of her journal. It is clear, first, that she is an American woman. Second, that from her early years, maybe [at] seventeen or eighteen, she became increasingly ill, so that little by little all of the normal activities of her life were cut off, and after many experiences she discovered that what she had lost in her lack of excursions into the outer world, freedom of movement, and so forth, she began to find balance by the kinds of excursions which she more and more was able to take by exploring the landscape within herself.[10] She kept a journal. About eight years after her illness she became acquainted with the mystics and began studying them very carefully, and perhaps she was more deeply influenced by Evelyn Underhill than by any other person or book save her excursions into the New Testament and the impact of the life of Jesus upon her.[11] Now that is as much as the book reveals about who she was and about the statistics of her life.[12]

Now I'd like to have you explore her mind and spirit for a little. You will bear in mind the basic thesis upon which we are working during this

---

10. Steger had limited vision and hearing, and in addition to those "incurable and slowly increasing handicaps" she also suffered from "neurasthenia" on the "journey of mine in affliction" (Stannard, "Margaret Prescott Montague," and Steger, *Leaves,* 9).

11. Evelyn Underhill (1875–1941) was a leading authority on mysticism, best known for *Mysticism: A Study in the Nature and Development of Man's Spiritual Consciousness* (London: Methuen, 1911). For Thurman on Underhill, see HT, "Mysticism and Social Change," #14, 27 July 1978, part of a course Thurman taught at the Pacific School of Religion. Steger mentions reading "one of Evelyn Underhill's books" (120), and makes special reference to her introduction to the *Songs of Kabir* (New York: Macmillan, 1915), a translation of the fifteenth-century Indian songs of Kabir by Rabindranath Tagore (55). (Thurman quotes from the same book in a sermon from 1925 [PHWT 1: 51].) Steger also mentions mystics discussed by Underhill, the fourteenth-century German mystic Heinrich Suso, St. Catherine of Siena, and the English metaphysical poet Thomas Traherne (61, 81). Steger also makes two references to William James's *Varieties of Religious Experience* (119, 131).

12. Thurman chose not to mention another aspect of Steger's biography that *Leaves from a Secret Journal* makes clear, that she was a wealthy white Southern woman, with a stereotyped and patronizing view of African Americans. Steger writes that there was a "mysterious something, value, beauty, ecstasy, *otherwhereness*" more frequent in Blacks than whites, "perhaps because they are more primitive," with less artifice, something she had observed in the "long procession of Negro servants in our family" (96–98).

series. That there is a spirit that is Creator and creative of which the external world is a manifestation. That the manifestation of the creative spirit of the Creator seems best exemplified in the things that we recognize as conscious things, things that are from within a narrow compass, things that are living things like trees and cats and dogs and people. That there is in man, and some even say in all living things, that which is not an expression of the Creator but that which *is* the Creator himself. That there is, to borrow a phrase from one about whom we shall be thinking in two weeks, there is in every living thing an uncreated element, a core that *is*, that is not becoming; that is not on the make, that is not potential but *is*.[13] This Isness is God, say these mystics. If I want to find him, then I need not, of necessity, go yonder, but all I need do is turn within, that he is in me already; that the disciplines of the spirit have as their fundamental purpose the widening of the area of the domination of the God that is within us. Caught in that concept, these mystics deal with various aspects of human experience: life, death, suffering, birth, all of the various things in which we are involved.

Now with that broad and rather sketchy but basic outline of the position of these mystics with whom we have been dealing over the past few weeks, let us look at Jane Steger. She begins with the simple feeling really that all of creation is alive; that just behind the tree is what she calls the spirit of the tree.[14] Now she's all right. There is nothing wrong with her. She is not a pantheist either, but we need not concern ourselves with these learned phrases.[15] She feels that the living thing in her, the something in her, is not unlike the living thing that is in the trees, in the flowers and so forth. There are times when she tries to relate, to let these two things which are the same thing get together. She goes outwards and looks at the tree and does whatever her sort of mind and spirit do with reference to the tree. She has moments when she is sure that she can hear the tree growing, [but] not in the sense that they do in Iowa about the corn. (When I was in Iowa one summer, at midnight, a friend of mine took me way outside of Iowa City and parked by a big cornfield. He said, "Now you listen very

---

13. "Men Who Have Walked with God: Meister Eckhart," XI, 5 July 1953.
14. For Steger's discussion of the secrets of trees, see *Leaves*, 78–88.
15. "I wish Eastern thought, much of which I like so much, did not go over into what appears to be pure pantheism. . . . The little spark of individuality that is myself digs in against such thought" (Steger, *Leaves*, 16–17).

carefully, and if you do, it's so hot you can hear the corn growing." But we didn't. We simply heard crickets.) But what she is saying is that she can feel the life in another living thing. I remember visiting in a home once where the lady of the house was taking care of her flowers. She said to me, "I water my flowers and I give them some of these synthetic things, but that isn't the thing that makes my flowers grow. I love my flowers. I brood over my flowers. I give them something to which they respond; something in the flower responds to something in me. When that happens, then they *have* to grow."[16] Does that sound stupid? No, I don't think so. But anyway, that's the way she goes at it. Now she applies the same thing to human beings. She talks about the "winks" of beauty that she sees in various kinds of human beings. This something in them is trying to break through, to announce itself to the whole world, but the human being is so burdened by fears, so burdened by hate sometimes, burdened by pain, by miseries, by frustrations, by internal disorders and churnings that this thing is blocked, and it can't get through to express itself. And she says, "Sometimes when it does get through, illumination takes place." She has a great chapter on light and how when something in the individual permits him to relax his anxieties and fears, he seeks to attune himself with the God that is in him; then his countenance becomes illumined. It's the light, she says, that one feels rather than a light that one sees.[17]

Now a second aspect of her insight is that, for a long time, every day was a monotonous sort of routine thing. Then as she began her meditations and her prayers, one of the things that occurred to her was that she was just not expecting anything. She said that life is surrounded by so many little expressions of wholeness, of winged messengers, but we don't see them pass. While I was sitting here reflecting on all of this a few minutes ago, my eyes fell on something right here. Now it is a Mr. and Mrs. Ronkey, September 25, 1932.[18] Now I have been sitting here nearly five years and this is the first time I've seen it. Looking, looking straight, because I cannot see anything but this; but I sit every Sunday

---

16. Thurman taught at the University of Iowa in Iowa City in the summer of 1948.
17. Steger, *Leaves*, 109–42.
18. In 1949 Fellowship Church purchased the former home of St. John's Evangelical and Reformed Church. The Ronkeys presumably were commemorated on a plaque on the pulpit, which Thurman had not previously noticed.

and I haven't seen it, and when I saw it then my mind began moving over all of the things that must have been at work. Who were these people? What kind of contribution they must have made to the Evangelical and Reformed Church which was here that would cause people in the congregation to wish to identify their spirit with the place from which the Book would be read Sunday after Sunday? And a good feeling that I was a part of the human race that could feel such things and do such things simply swept all over me. Now that's what she's talking about. I didn't know that I would have so perfect an experience of it in my own life sitting right before you, but she's saying that once I'm on the look, once I am open, once I become increasingly aware of these overtones then every day is fuller in the most unexpected places.

About five months ago, at the close of the morning's service, a man who was seated down front came up and he said, "I want to tell you a miracle that I saw just now." He said that when the congregation stood and we began singing the closing hymn, "I found myself looking at the flowers and before my eyes I saw a bud burst out into flower." He was just sitting there looking. That was all. We are surrounded by it. As Alfred Noyes suggests in *Watchers of the Sky,* "There is magic all around us, in the rocks, in the trees, in the mind of men; deep hidden springs of magic, and he who strikes the rocks aright may find it where he will."[19] We are surrounded by it.

Now a third thing out of her life which is very important. When she began praying and exploring the inner depths of her own spirit, getting these glimpses of God and these deep insights with reference to him, she was frightened. And she was frightened because she said I can't follow up on that. I dare not surrender my life to God. I dare not give myself

---

19. Alfred Noyes, *Watchers of the Skies* (New York: Frederick A. Stokes, 1922), 65. The quote:

    There's magic all around us
    In rocks and trees, and in the minds of men
    Deep hidden springs of magic
    He that strikes
    The rock aright, may find them
       Where he will.

This was one of Thurman's favorite quotations. Noyes (1880–1958) was an English poet. *Watchers of the Skies* was a book-length poem on the Copernican revolution.

over to the moving spirit that more and more is being disclosed within me because, said she, if I do, God will require of me something that is so unusual and so dramatic that I don't think I can do it. I am afraid. Suppose he asks me—she's very shy—suppose he asks me to stand on the street corner and preach. Suppose he asks me—she gives an illustration of the Salvation Army ladies who at Christmastime ring the bell over the pot. She said that I would just be horrified with my kind of shyness and embarrassment to stand there and do that. Suppose God asked me to do something like that and then I would have to go back on my word; but indeed I couldn't go back on my word, and how terrible it would be to know that I had lied to God. But finally, she said, I overcame it, and to my amazement God did not ask me to do anything like that. He just asked me to clean out my bureau drawers and to get a lot of little things in order and to do certain simple things with reference to my mother with whom I was living. All these little ways. And then she said I remembered how for so long a time I had held back from him because I was afraid that if I did not, he would make me do something that would stretch me completely out of shape.[20]

Then there's a fourth thing. She has some interesting insight about human suffering; a rather practical thing, almost winsome. She writes in her journal some of the feelings when the doctor told her that the possibilities are that she would get increasingly worse rather than better. How she dealt with that in her own mind and spirit, and she found that the thing that paralyzed her most of all was not suffering itself but the fear of suffering. She had to overcome that. She spent many hours in prayer and meditation seeking to get a perspective on her condition. And interestingly, nowhere in the pages is there anything about getting her condition changed. Getting the facts shifted. Getting a perspective on it. Which is very interesting. And she says, "In my imagination I think that human beings are to God as the fingers are to the hand; that some of the fingers are the fingers through which God hurts, God suffers, and that the people who come to earth, perhaps," she says, "they may ask before they are born, they may volunteer to be God's fingers of suffering."[21] It seemed far-fetched, perhaps, doesn't it? But that's a great concept. In Deutero-Isaiah,

---

20. Steger, *Leaves*, 72–73
21. "I sometimes think that we are to God as his fingers are to a blind person. Through us He feels of life in all of its manifold experiences. . . . The fingers and the

you remember, the concept of the suffering servant, that of all the vast movement of human beings across all of the pages of history, only Israel, says Deutero-Isaiah, was chosen by Yahweh to reveal to life and to all the ages of man the insights that can only come from the broken heart and the crushed spirit.[22] The finger, the finger of God's suffering. For she feels in a very simple way, that if God could not suffer, then there could be no consciousness either of God or there would be no consciousness of God in us. It is a rather interesting thing, but the basic insight is sound. It takes suffering—this is the insight—it takes suffering out of the category of the negative. It takes suffering out of the category of mere divine vengeance, of divine revelation; but it places suffering in the point of the experience that gives to the *experiencer* of the suffering the possibility of distilling out of it something that he could get in no other way. It is an interesting thing, and she is not by herself in what she does with the subject.

Now one other thing. She borrows a phrase from William Blake. A phrase which is this: the death of the divine image.[23] And this is what she says about it. Bear in mind about her whole idea of the consciousness of God expressing in all of these manifold ways. Every time I do a good, wholesome, spontaneous act of response to human need in self-giving, every time I do that, a part of the divine image is sacrificed in the act. That when I share my life outgoing to meet the needs of someone else, I participate, at that point, in the death of the divine image; that is, the sacrifice of the divine image in the act by which the need in another person is redeemed. She says, "I participate in the birth of the divine image when I am able to make to God a whole offering of my life, whether it is my pain, my joy; whether it is my dreams, my hopes, my anxieties, my fears; whatever it is that I am able to offer completely to God, in that offering I participate in the birth of the divine image in me."[24]

And now, to put it together. She feels that the line that separates the two worlds is a very thin line. That there is thus a door between. That

---

palm of the hand seem to me to be a good symbol of our relationship with God" (Steger, *Leaves*, 51).

22. Isaiah 52:13–53:15.

23. "Every kindness to another is a little death in the Divine Image" (William Blake, "Jerusalem," stanza 96, l. 25; Steger, *Leaves*, 25–29).

24. Steger, *Leaves*, 25–29. Thurman is loosely paraphrasing, not quoting, Steger.

door is in the heart.[25] That we find ourselves going through that door and then coming back on this side. There is something very profound; that we are like the blind puppy. It's a wonder. I wish I had time to read it to you. The puppy is blind when he is born, and he needs to sniff all the time. He sniffs everything. And he has an idea that that's all, that for the rest of his life he will have to be guided by his nose, exclusively. And then one day, his eyes open, and he sees all the world that he did not dream of as existing when he was in the blind, sniffing stage. Now, she says, that, that is where we are. We are in the blind puppy stage.[26] We are using our minds as equivalent to the way the puppy uses his nose, and we feel that everything that is anything can be grasped by our little minds; that if it doesn't make sense to the mind then it has no sense at all. We are in the blind puppy stage, sniffing all over the place with our little intellects. But she says that there will come a time when our eyes will open as indeed she said in everybody's experience, there are moments when the eye does open and many things that I cannot grasp with my mind disclose themselves to me in a quality of assurance and conviction that is far more important than all the logic that I can muster.

It is like the experience of Tolstoy, standing in the public square, and he sees a man beheaded; and as the man's head falls in the empty wicker basket on the other side, Tolstoy says, "that a level in me, deeper than thought, deeper than logic, deeper than my culture, deeper than my religious conviction, I knew that this thing was wrong."[27] Now it happens to us.

---

25. "Often for days and weeks the doors of the spirit have been tight shut against me.... I open door after door, and all the chambers are empty and desolate... but oh, think of the dancing, Heaven-sent days, when the doors are wide open, and life is one golden stream of love!" (Steger, *Leaves*, 5).

26. Steger, *Leaves*, 20.

27. Thurman is paraphrasing from Tolstoy's *A Confession*, where he documents his early revolt against "superstitious belief in progress." The actual quote is: "When I saw the head part from the body and how they thumped separately into the box, I understood, not with my mind but with my whole being, that no theory of the reasonableness of our present progress could justify this deed; and that though everybody from the creation of the world had held it to be necessary, on whatever theory, I knew it to be unnecessary and bad; and therefore the arbiter of what is good and evil is not what people say and do, nor is it progress, but it is my heart and I" (*A Confession, and the Spirit of Christ's Teaching* [London: T. Y Crowell, 1887], 14).

MEISTER ECKHART

5 July 1953
Fellowship Church

The German mystic and Dominican theologian Eckhart von Hochheim, or Johannes Eckhart, better known as Meister Eckhart (ca. 1260–1327), was born near Gotha in Thuringia and studied and taught in the major Dominican schools, notably at Paris, Strasbourg, and Cologne, and held a series of offices in his order.[1] Eckhart's teachings influenced a movement of mystical leaders in fourteenth-century Germany, which included Johannes Tauler (1300–1361) and Heinrich Suso (1295–1366). Of all of the figures Thurman discussed in the "Men Who Have Walked with God" series, no one was more significant in his intellectual development than Eckhart, who had been a special interest of Thurman since the 1920s. Thurman here claims that one of his most important social ideas, the "infinite worth" of every individual, was derived from Eckhart's notion that "there is central in every living person a core which has at its core the eternally undifferentiated Godhead."[2]

Thurman participated in an advanced seminar on Eckhart with Rufus Jones at Haverford College in 1929.[3] In 1934 Thurman offered to speak at

---

For Thurman's previous use of the quotation in his 1939 lecture series "Mysticism and Social Change," see PHWT 2: 207.

1. For Thurman's other writings on Eckhart, see "The Inward Journey III: Meister Eckhart: From Whom God Hid Nothing," 15 October 1961; and two lectures Thurman delivered at the University of Redlands in a spring 1973 course on mysticism.

2. The German Romantic philosopher Franz von Baader (1765–1841), who was largely responsible for the renewed interest in Eckhart after centuries of relative neglect, and who, with his friend Georg Wilhelm Friedrich Hegel, undertook an intensive study of Eckhart in the 1820s, argued that one of his insights was the recognition of the infinite worth of the individual; Cyril O'Regan, *The Heterodox Hegel* (Albany: SUNY Press, 1994), 251. For Thurman on infinite worth, see "Freedom under God," in PHWT 4: 112–20.

3. WHAH 76.

a conference on Eckhart, the same year he wrote of Eckhart in a review of Mary Anita Ewer's Survey of Mystical Symbolism.[4] *He also had multiple references to Eckhart in his 1939 lectures "Mysticism and Social Change."*[5] *For Thurman, Eckhart was, as he was known in his lifetime, "the man from whom God hid nothing,"*[6] *and whose thinking he admired for the boldness of his religious formations.*

Thurman adopts the analogy of a spring that "spills over" in the lives of others to describe Eckhart's creative and revolutionary spirituality: "When the Godhead manifests itself, when the Godhead becomes in any dimension self-conscious, then God is born. . . . If when any of the water of the spring spills over, that spilling in Eckhart's thought is God. You can see the spill, you can deal with the spill: it separates itself somewhat from the spring itself." This movement of the Spirit, says Thurman, results in a logic that "spills over in time and space; therefore when the Godhead which is at the core of me spills over in my time-space relationships, at least I can say that wherever such a person is there the kingdom of God is at hand."

I want to read a little poem.

>Hemmed in by petty thoughts and petty things,
>Intent on toys and trifles all my years,
>Pleased by life's gauds, pained by its pricks and stings,
>Swayed by ignoble hopes, ignoble fears;
>Threading life's tangled maze without life's clue,
>Busy with means, yet heedless of their ends,
>Lost to all sense of what is real and true,
>Blind to the goal to which all Nature tends: —

---

4. HT to Dorothy Phillips, Loma Linda, CA, 21 November 1934; review of 21 November 1934 of Mary Anita Ewer, *Survey of Mystical Symbolism,* in PHWT 1: 203–4.

5. "Mysticism and Social Change," PHWT 2: 197, 203.

6. The title dates to the fourteenth century. Eckhart's sermons were prepared by his students. Sermon 1 is titled "This Is Meister Eckhart from Whom God Hid Nothing"; *Meister Eckhart: A Modern Translation* (trans. Raymond B. Blakney; New York: Harper & Brothers, 1941), 95.

Such is my surface self: but deep beneath,
A mighty actor on a world-wide stage,
Crowned with all knowledge, lord of life and death,
Sure of my aim, sure of my heritage,—
I—the true self—live on, in self's despite,
That "life profound" whose darkness is God's light.[7]

This is a continuation of our series Men Who Have Walked with God, Meister Eckhart, concerning whom it was said, "From him God hid nothing." Eckhart dramatizes, in my own thinking at any rate, one of the interesting and significant paradoxes that we find in studying the history of mystical thought, certainly as far as Western culture and Western civilization are concerned: for some of the most profoundly influential mystics, those who seemingly have plumbed depths which leave the rest of us high on the shore, were nurtured in the bosom of Roman Catholicism, in the bosom of a church that is carefully structured; a church that is in some rather significant ways authoritarian; a church which has its categories fairly well and fairly accurately defined, and yet within the bosom of—I do not speak irreverently or whatever the other word is now—but a church which is fundamentally authoritarian as any institution would be that had had a monopoly for a thousand years.[8] That is not a criticism of Roman Catholicism; it is simply a fact in social evolution, of which it has taken good advantage. But there it is. In some ways a rigid system, a church that is officially the dispenser of the medicine of salvation, with the medicine of salvation expressing itself or spelled out in terms of the

---

7. "La vie profounde," by Edmond Gore Alexander Holmes (1850–1936), an English author on spiritual topics, whose religious thought tended to pantheistic spiritualism.

8. Criticisms of Roman Catholicism as a basically totalitarian institution were common among progressive liberals and liberal Protestants in the late 1940s and early 1950s. The best-known polemics on the subject were Paul Blanshard's *American Freedom and Catholic Power* (Boston: Beacon Press, 1949) and *Communism, Democracy, and Catholic Power* (Boston: Beacon Press, 1951)

seven sacraments.[9] And yet within that framework, there has grown up through the years, nurtured in its very bosom—to mix the metaphor—these daring spirits, the logic of whose insight is to transcend and ultimately negate any institution that undertakes to introduce the human soul to its Gods. It is an amazing thing. But they almost caught Eckhart.[10] How he got by I don't quite know, but they didn't put some of his things on the index until after he was dead.[11] He had narrow skirmishes, and I think he had these narrow skirmishes because he was a man with a highly developed mind and a disciplined spirit who spoke in a language that communicated itself to the masses of the people. I think that is really the reason why he had so much trouble. He was thoroughly trained, thoroughly disciplined, but he preached not out of his mind but out of his heart. And heart responded to heart in a way that was independent of sacrament, independent of institution.[12]

Now when you read Eckhart's sermons today you wonder what kind of people were just lay people back in the thirteenth century, because when you read his sermons it is very difficult to understand what on earth he is talking about unless you get inside and look out, and we don't

---

9. The seven sacraments of the Catholic Church are baptism, confirmation, Eucharist, penance, anointing of the sick, marriage, and holy orders.

10. Thurman is referring to Eckhart's eventual trial for heresy, which took place between August 1325 and September 1326 in Cologne, Germany. He was charged with errors relating to the concept of divine filiation, the relation between God and world, the Trinity, divine birth, negative theology, the soul, universals, prayer, and interpretation of the Bible, among the twenty-eight articles used in the inquisition. His disciples' petitions to have the decree removed were in vain. Eckhart died in 1327 before John XXII issued a bull in 1329 condemning seventeen of Eckhart's propositions as heretical.

11. Although some of Eckhart's propositions were condemned by the church shortly after his death, the infamous Index of Prohibited Books, the *Index Librorum Prohibitorum,* was not created until 1559. It was abolished in 1966.

12. Eckhart's preaching to the common people in German is sometimes referred to as "vernacular theology." In his defense against charges of heresy, he proclaimed, "And we shall be told that no one is to talk about or write such teachings to the untaught. But to this I say if we are not to teach people who have not been taught, no one will ever be taught, and no one will ever be able to teach and write. For that is why we teach the untaught so that they will be changed from uninstructed to instructed." See *Meister Eckhart: The Essential Sermons, Commentaries, Treatises and Defense* (ed. Edmund Colledge and Bernard McGinn; Mahwah, NJ: Paulist Press, 1981), 239.

read that way. We read outside and look outside. But at any rate wherever Eckhart opened his mouth to preach the little people crowded the place. What was he talking about? Let's examine the basis of his mysticism for a few minutes and see what instructions there may be for us.

Eckhart stated that the ground of all existence was what he called the Godhead. Now, don't trouble yourself too much about the terms, just feel along. The Godhead. The Godhead in Eckhart's language is that which is at the ground of all manifestations of life. It is without classification, without differentiation, without division.[13] It sustains, supports all manifestations; but it, itself, is a continuum in which there is no movement. It cannot be named, for if you name it you limit it. It is the "nameless nothing," he says.[14] (That's a nice word.) The "unnatured nature," another phrase he uses desperately trying to say that you can't say it, you see, and he does it creatively. Now, that's the Godhead.

When the Godhead manifests itself, when the Godhead becomes in any dimension self-conscious, then God is born. This is the best way I can describe this to you; here is a spring, and we will call the spring the Godhead. When any of the water of the spring spills over, that spilling in Eckhart's thought is God. You can see the spill, you can deal with the spill: it separates itself somewhat from the spring itself.

Now, the Son is the act. (It is very complicated, perhaps, but not so much.) The Son is the act by which God becomes aware of himself. God looking back upon himself is the Son. The relationship [is] between God as the spilling over, [and] the differentiation of the Godhead and [this] process by which this spilling over takes on the form of consciousness. Wherever there is consciousness there is subject and object. And this

---

13. See Bernard McGinn, *The Mystical Thought of Meister Eckhart: The Man from Whom God Hid Nothing* (New York: Crossroad Publishing, 2001), chapter 3, "Eckhart and the Mysticism of the Ground." McGinn understands *grunt* to be a "master metaphor that is also an explosive metaphor that breaks through old categories, inviting the hearer to perform the same breakthrough in life."

14. "Now pay attention to this. God is nameless for no one can either speak of him or know him. Therefore a pagan master says that what we can know or say of the First Cause reflects ourselves more than it does the First Cause, for this transcends all speech and all understanding.... He is being beyond being: he is a nothingness beyond being" (Sermon 96, Meister Eckhart, *Selected Writings* (ed. and trans. Oliver Davies; London: Penguin Press, 1994), 236.

whole creative relationship between subject and object into which the Godhead breaks in differentiation is the Holy Spirit. Well, we need not bother too much with the theology of it, but that's the way his mind goes. That bottoming all form, all movement, all nature, all activity, all existence, and all existences is this undifferentiated ground of being. Only he wouldn't say "of being"; that's a mistake, because the minute I say "of being," I limit it, and he wouldn't limit this ground, period.

Now, the Creator of the world, the Creator of matter, the Creator of all things, all existences is not the Godhead. It is God, that which becomes differentiated. And in God's mind—you see the influence of Plotinus and the influence of Plato and the influence of some other people in the thinking of Eckhart—for in the mind of God the Creator, who is the personal God, the spilling over of the Godhead in time and space that all creations, every object that we experience, is but a manifestation of certain archetypes. To illustrate it as we did when we were talking about Plotinus weeks ago,[15] the spirit, the—well, your cat, Josephine may die and your neighbor's cat, Henry, may die, but cats don't die. Cats keep coming on. Individual men may die, but Man doesn't die.

Now, what he is saying is that man as an archetype, as an idea, exists in the mind of God and keeps spilling out eternally. Therefore, the reality, pushed you see, the reality is not in the particular manifestation, but the reality is behind that: the eternal thing of which the particular that we experience is a manifestation. Well, so much for that part of it.

Now, the most significant part of his insight—and you are doing very well; you haven't just deserted me yet. The second part of it, and which is perhaps, certainly from my point of view, the most important part, is what he has to say about the soul. I read a contemporary poem from this book of mystical verse in which there is a division between the lower self and the higher self. It is a division which Eckhart makes, and he makes in a very striking manner. The lower self is the self of the senses. It is the means by which we communicate in the world of senses, of sense experience. It is the dimension of attachment. It is the area, the [milieu] from which we draw all of our collections of fears and hopes and dreams, aspirations, yearnings; all of the vaulting ambitions of the human spirit,

---

15. See "Men Who Have Walked with God: Plotinus," printed in the current volume.

all of the things upon which we lay hold with abiding enthusiasms and clutch them saying, "This is mine, and mine forever and mine alone." All of the ways by which we give to ourselves the assurances that nullify the deep sense of isolation of the human spirit. That is the surface self, says Eckhart.

Now, there is another self. There is another division. Eckhart, of course, calls this second division—even uses the word "the unconscious," but I dare not use that word. It is loaded. And I won't do that, but Eckhart called it the unconscious. It is also the ground, which is identical with this ground that he calls the Godhead, you see. That there is in me, and this is his great contribution, there is in me the same ground that is the Godhead. There is another self that he calls sometimes the "active reason," which is [another] dimension of the self, [which has at its] core the "uncreated element." It is God, it is the Godhead, it is the expression—not the expression, how to say this—it's the isness of the Godhead itself. It is not broken down in any form, but it is the center of the core of my being, which core is central to the active reason.

Now Eckhart says, when I want to find my true self, I do not chase up and down the highways of my senses for they lead me consistently astray. But when I want to find my true self, I disentangle myself from the senses, from this other region and move straight to the core of me. Which, says Eckhart, is where the Godhead is located. Therefore, there is in the soul of man that which is uncreated, which has never been created, which is the Godhead itself. And the individual, and he was almost a pantheist here, the individual can retreat from the senses; retreat until finally he becomes one with this core, but not quite. Eckhart is not quite an Oriental,[16] you see, for he says that the soul of man does not quite merge, become one, with the Godhead.

Now, says Eckhart, the way by which this core, this Godhead which is the uncreated element at the very core, the way [by] which the individual grows in spiritual awareness, the way by which the individual grows in spiritual stature and in richness is to do the things that will widen the area of the spread of this uncreated element which is at the core of one's being, of one's soul. And how do you do that? You do that by, first of all,

---

16. That is, Thurman was saying that Eckhart had certain affinities with Eastern philosophies such as Buddhism or Hinduism but remained distinct.

by working on detachment. And he comes back, you see, to his wrestle with the senses. No man who is involved in attachments can free himself so as to give, to keep from blocking the spread of the Godhead which is [in him] the core of his soul in his life. So, the only way by which you can precipitate this spread is by disentangling the self from all the things that commit the mind and commit the spirit and involve the heart.

Now, he sounds as if he is altogether negative, but he isn't, for he says—he is full of surprises—he says that if a man is having the most profound kind of mystical experience, as St. Paul had when he was carried into the third heaven [2 Corinthians 12:2], and there in the midst of that highly accentuated moment of divine awareness he remembers that there is some man around the corner who is hungry. He had better leave his mystical experience and go and feed him and then come back. And that is all right, isn't it?

Another time, one of the interesting anecdotes about him, or stories about him, he was walking through the streets with a lantern in the daytime. And then he finally found a man who asked him—he had a lantern in one hand and a bucket of water in the other hand—and the man said, "What are you going to do with these things, Meister Eckhart?" He said, "Well, with the water I am going to put hell out, and with the lantern I am going to burn heaven up so that men will serve God because they love him rather than because," well, for the obvious reasons.

Now, there is a very interesting and searching ethic that is derived from Eckhart; if it be true as Eckhart presupposes, assumes, believes, and affirms that there is central in every living person a core which has at its core the eternally undifferentiated Godhead, then that means two things that are very important. One: that I am never permitted to say of another human being that he is anything that is a denial of the infinite worth of his personality, because his personality is the basket in which is carried this priceless ingredient. And I can never deal with another human being as if he is just another human being. He is carrying around with him this uncreated element—and therefore, in all of my primary, intimate face-to-face or secondary contacts with human beings my greatest and most insistent responsibility is to seek to develop with them the kind of relationships that will make it possible for core to salute core. The core in me to salute the core in you. And any attitude that I have that stops it, any mood that I have that makes it difficult, any involvements of my life however holy they may be that will block it, these must be destroyed [so] that the core in me may be able to salute the core in you. That is the business of man. And when he does it, he becomes in that moment a manifestation of the Godhead. He spills over. And Eckhart even goes so far at one time to say that such a human being becomes God. But he took it back when they put too much pressure on him. But you see the logic of it: that if the Godhead becomes God when it spills over in time and space, therefore when the Godhead which is at the core of me spills over in my time-space relationships, at least I can say that wherever such a person is there the kingdom of God is at hand. At least we can say that much.

Now, sin for Eckhart is not so much how people behave; he doesn't ignore it, don't misunderstand me, but sin in Eckhart is self-will. It is when the will deliberately blocks the light, the manifestations of this uncreated core in personality. Now, this means that there is within the power of the individual with his mind to cover over this uncreated element. But it is not within the power of any individual to destroy this. This is very important. And you can see the revolutionary character of the doctrine about which he insists because if we say that it is not within the power of the individual, whatever may be the nature of his behavior to destroy, to nullify, to wipe out this uncreated element, then the logic of that is that no man under any circumstance can ultimately be cut off from God. And you can see what a doctrine like that would do, not to Catholicism merely of the thirteenth and fourteenth centuries but what it would do to contemporary Protestantism and Catholicism. That there is nothing that the individual can do that can destroy the Godhead that is within him.

JACOB BOEHME

12 July 1953
Fellowship Church

In the following sermon, after the opening meditation, Thurman reviews the life and message of Jacob Boehme (1575–1624), an influential and gifted Christian thinker and mystic born in Alt-Seidenberg near Görlitz, Saxony (now in Germany).[1] The fourth child of parents who were farmers, Jacob became a shoemaker after moving to Görlitz in 1599 and raising a family. He was not formally educated beyond elementary school, but possessed a keen faculty for observation and a voracious appetite for the intellectual and symbolic understanding of the life of the spirit. A Lutheran by birth and practice, he incorporated the doctrines and ideas associated with a train of thinkers related to the spiritual theology of Lutheranism.[2] Boehme claimed that he experienced mystical visions from childhood that recurred with greater frequency over the years. In 1612, he published his first treatise, Aurora, *a controversial writing of his mystical experiences of being "enwrapped in the Divine Light." This and other writings[3] eventually resulted in his expulsion from Görlitz by the town council. He resided in*

---

1. For Boehme, see John Joseph Stoudt, *Boehme: His Life and Thought* (New York: Seabury Press, 1968

2. Among these thinkers are Caspar Schwenkfeld von Ossig (1490–1561); Sebastian Franck, (1499–1542); Valentine Weigel (1533–1588), all influential figures in the Spiritual Reformist tradition that emphasized mystical attitude in place of dogmatic belief.

3. For a recent English edition of *Aurora*, see *The Way to Christ*, ed. and trans. Peter Erb (New York: Paulist Press, 1978). Boehme has been called "the new Valentinus," a reference to the second century CE gnostic, and credited with "a veritable efflorescence of Gnostic mythology" that influenced notable thinkers such as Johann Wolfgang von Goethe, Georg Wilhelm Friedrich Hegel, Friedrich Oetinger, and Franz von Baader. See Giovanni Filoramo, A *History of Gnosticism*, trans. Anthony Black (Cambridge and Oxford: Blackwell Publishers, 1994), xiv. Little of Boehme's work is available in recent English translations, but see *The Way to Christ*, trans. Peter C. Erb (New York:

Dresden, among a receptive community of intellectuals and shortly before his death returned to Görlitz.

Thurman spoke on Boehme on at least three occasions.[4] In this presentation, the reader gets a glimpse at Thurman's pedagogical method, which is always focused on education of both "head and heart." Thurman identifies two major secondary works on Boehme, which he suggests as sources for the congregation to further explore the life and message of this remarkable religious thinker who was a critical source for the birth of what is now known as Quakerism.[5] Boehme influenced Thurman on questions such as the problem of the universal and particular, the problem of religious knowledge, mystic union as involving the inner and outer dimensions of religious experience, and most importantly, the two wills.

According to Thurman, the complex problem of religious knowledge[6] in Boehme is rooted in the mystic's claim of union with the Divine, in which she or he must of necessity bring experience of the outer world of particulars into the inner state of union, which denotes universality. The danger of this position, Thurman suggests, is that if individuality is lost in the process of union,

---

Paulist Press, 1978); *The Signatures of All Things and Other Writings* (London: James Clark, 1969)

4. In addition to this sermon, see "Men Who Walked with God: Jacob Boehme," 3 July 1950; "The Mystic Will: Jacob Boehme," 8 October 8, 1961

5. Rufus Jones says of Boehme, "no more remarkable religious message has come in modern centuries from an untrained and undisciplined mind than that which lies scattered through the voluminous and somewhat chaotic writings of this seventeenth-century prophet of the common people," *Spiritual Reformers of the Sixteenth and Seventeenth Centuries* (New York: Macmillan, 1914), 153

6. In early December 1925, while a student at Rochester Theological Seminary Thurman wrote a paper entitled "Can It Be Truly Said That the Existence of a Supreme Spirit Is a Scientific Hypothesis?" PHWT 1: 54–67. In his paper, he argues that the scientific method simplifies the confused nature of external reality into quantifiable and testable hypotheses, but all knowledge gained in this way is necessarily provisional and cannot provide information about the ultimate nature of the physical universe. He concludes that only in the realm of religion is certain knowledge perhaps attainable through the possibility of experiential knowledge of God through heightened states of divine awareness. Thurman's paper set out several themes that he would return to throughout his career, a measured and rationalistic approach to knowledge claims on the one hand and holding out the possibility of non-rational knowledge of divine reality on the other. For a perspective that challenges Thurman's view of religious knowledge, see Victor Anderson, *Creative Exchange: A Constructive Theology of African American Religious Experience.* (Minneapolis, MN: Fortress Press, 2008), 123–24.

then how can one know that s/he is in union with the Divine? Thurman was acutely aware of the danger of subjectivism and privatization of meaning implied in the emphasis on the appeal to religious experience. He guarded against this tendency by accentuating the need for empirical verification of what one experiences in her or his inner life. "The real questions at issue here," he contends, "are, how may a man know he is not being deceived? Is there any way by which he may know beyond doubt, and therefore with verification, that what he experiences is authentic and genuine?"[7] Thurman thinks that it is possible as with Boehme's understanding of the two wills or what he sometimes calls "double vision" or "double view" (one focused on the external manifestation of the world in which particulars dominate and inform our claims to knowledge; and the inner will which focus on the eternal and universal which is true knowledge expressed in wholeness, completeness and truth) to gain a greater sense of the ethical and moral obligation to love.

To Keep from Being Destroyed by Hardness of Heart

The tidings that come to us through the air, by radio and television, the words that come to us from the printed page of the morning paper, give to our minds and our spirits ever insistent tidings of great and agonizing tragedies, death by the hundreds, death by the thousands, hunger in the hundreds, hunger in the thousands, tidings of tragedy beaten upon our minds and upon our spirits. And we protect ourselves from internal collapse and disorganization and panic by hardening our minds and hardening our hearts, so that our eyes as we glance at the page, our ears as

---

7. HT, *The Creative Encounter: An Interpretation of Religion and the Social Witness* (New York: Harper and Brothers, 1954), 57. Rational coherence between the inner experience of self and the social world is the method employed to test for self-deception. He argues, "Whatever seems to deny a fundamental structure of orderliness upon which rationality seems to depend cannot be countenanced" (57–58). See also Walter Earl Fluker, "Dangerous Memories and Redemptive Possibilities: Reflections on the Life and Work of Howard Thurman" in *Black Leaders and Ideologies in the South: Resistance and Nonviolence*, ed. Preston King and Walter Earl Fluker (London and New York: Routledge, Taylor Francis Group, 2005), 167.

we listen, will not say to us the height and depth of the private and collective misery of our fellows. In our private lives the same thing seems to be true so often; each one of us, as he looks at his own life, the way in which he is involved in the lives of others, he identifies with their suffering, with their disaster, even as each one wrestles with his own suffering and own disaster in order that he may keep some sense of balance, and often that he may not become a stark, raving, maniac with reason dethroned. We school ourselves in looking the other way. There is only so much misery we can abide, and after that the lights go out.

So characteristic is this of the common life in which we are engaged, whether we contemplate ourselves and our neighbors, or the great drama that is taking place on the worldwide stage that involves us, that the danger and peril of hardness of heart and hardness of mind escapes us. If the heart is hard, if the mind has built a great wall of immunity against the anguish and cries of the world, there is no opening for the spirit of man to breathe, and the house in which he has hidden from the agony of the world becomes for him the house of death. And thus we are caught, caught by the agonizing grapple of the madness of our time, and the insistent insurgence of an all-pervasive identity with all of life, and in the quietness as we sit here, perhaps we may get some fleeting glimpse, some clue by which we may live in the world, sensitive to its needs and our own needs, and not be choked by despair, some fleeting insight into how the heart can break and continue to breathe as one heart.

O God, gather into thy spirit, the needs of our spirit, lest we wither on the vine and there shall be no life in us. O God, O God our Father, Amen.

If you are interested in reading about Jacob Boehme, and you do not wish to wade through the complicated writing that he left behind, I would suggest two references.[8] And I apologize that I haven't been doing this before, but it just occurred to me this morning that it might be a good idea. The first reference is: *The Mystic Will* by [Howard Haines] Brinton.[9]

---

8. The beginning of this sermon is lost. Thurman's opening mediation was on the "peril of hardness of hurt—protection from the violence of our time."

9. Howard Haines Brinton, *Mystic Will: Based Upon a Study of the Philosophy of Jacob Boehme* (New York: Macmillan, 1930). Howard Haines Brinton (1884–1973)

Dr. Brinton is one of the moving spirits, directors, of Pendle Hill which is the Quaker School of graduate study where Dr. Phelps is lecturing during the summer.[10] *The Mystic Will,* by Brinton. It's a Macmillan book and it is out of print, but you can find it in almost any good second hand book store if you go there often enough over a long enough time interval. The second reference is the Rufus Jones, *Spiritual Reformers of the Sixteenth and Seventeenth Centuries,*[11] I think is the title of it. *Spiritual Reformers* is the title. That book also is out of print but and you will not be fortunate to pick it up in a casual bookstore. You may pick it up in a highly specialized bookstore. I, myself, have been trying to find it for six years, but you still may be able to get it. In that study by Rufus Jones there are three very crucial chapters on Jacob Boehme.

Now—it is rather difficult to interpret his mystical insight without becoming far more involved in aspects of the discussion which from the point of view of our quest and our concern are irrelevant. I would like to therefore, begin by pointing up the central problem of mystical religion as that problem has expressed itself in our thought, and then to see how the mind of a man like Boehme moves in upon this problem and resolves it in a manner that seems to him to be very significant and resolves it in a manner that is so significant that he, perhaps more than any other person may be regarded as the womb out of which Quakerism comes.

There is a tendency in the human spirit, more than a tendency, an activity of the human spirit that moves always outward towards the world of things, the world of matter. It seeks always to understand the individual thing, the particular thing. It is characteristic of our civilization our western culture. We want to understand the world of nature and every aspect of the world of nature in order that we may be able from within the context of our understanding of nature control nature and make nature our servant. So ardent is this quest on our part and so successful have we been in the

---

was a professor and author of over a dozen books and pamphlets on Quakerism. He and his wife Anna Brinton served as directors of the Pendle Hill Friends Center in Wallington, PA from 1936 to 1952. For Howard Brinton's friendship with Thurman, see PWHT 2: 189

10. For Dryden Phelps, see "Men Who Walked with God; Lao-Tse" printed in this volume.

11. In the sermon, Thurman mistakenly called the book *Spiritual Reformers of the Fourteenth Century.*

pursuit of the quest that—pursuit in the quest that the significance of the individual, the man who is questing, has been lost sight of. Very interesting.

I saw a little skit on television that arrested my mind. I can't tell you how it ends because I've forgotten and I blacked out on it, but it was a skit having to do with what has happened to man and the machine. Perhaps something of this sort: all of the machines in the world suddenly decided that they would get rid of human beings, they were tired of being pushed around by men. So, the typewriters that had been obeying these stenographers all day just decided that they would move on the offensive, and they ran all of the stenographers out of the offices. The wires in the telephone got tired of responding and being a tool of these human manipulators, and these wires ran amuck and began twisting and turning and getting out of hand and choking and destroying. They were tired of man's petty domination. And the climax came when a man ran up three, four, five flights of stairs and staggered through a door on the roof and slammed the door and bolted it because he was trying to escape the adding machine.

But the concept is very interesting. It points up this thing that has happened in our [times]. [This is] the outgoing will. And that brings us to one of the insights of Boehme, but we will postpone it for a second. The way this outgoing will has sought always to understand the particular, and if I can understand enough particulars then out of that understanding of this collection of particulars, I will therefore get a total understanding of the whole. And yet the thing that blocks that is that there is a sense in which every particular, though it may not be different from some other particular yet is unique in itself. Every time I hit one of these I know that in order to be sure that my understanding, that my knowledge are complete, I must deal with every particular for ever and ever (and I can't do that) with the result that the particulars begin to take me over. Now, that is one push.

Now the other push in the human spirit is to move back in the other direction. This is as old, of course, as the problems of philosophy having to do with the universal and the particular, the general and the specific etc. Now, we move away from the world, boring always more deeply within: withdrawing until perhaps we come to some central core, some pulse out of which everything else emanates. But the problem always is that I cannot be aware that I am there, when I am at the core unless some part of me, some part of this outer is along with me to inform me of the fact that it is different from the thing I am experiencing. Do you see what I mean? [laughter] No, you don't.

Now, let's try it again. You see, when we say for instance that I will withdraw from the world, which is part of the mystic's insight, I will withdraw from the world and will become detached more and more so that there will be no thread of involvement at any point in order that I might plunge myself more deeply and utterly into the undifferentiated ground. When I move from the outer to the inner as long as there is some recollection of the outer in my experience, I can then be aware of the fact that I am aware of the inner: but if there is no outer with me then I cannot be aware of the inner. To state it in terms of religion, I know that I must go before God, that I must be washed of all of the things that delimit my life so that I can be utterly and completely acceptable in his sight. But if some part of me is not, some part of thisness is not with me in His presence, I cannot be identified and I must be identified.

Now, Jacob Boehme wrestles with this problem. And he begins with a very interesting concept. I should say that his dates are sixteenth century, sometime after 1500 and he was a Lutheran. He was a great Protestant and he was a visionary. He saw double all the time, you know, he saw double, wonderful! They thought he was a little strange and yet there were many people in his period who felt that way because the time was an uneasy time. And when the times are uneasy times then the stability of the human spirit has to be—in the preciseness of its vision something has to hold and let the ebb and flow of the eventful vicissitudes do all the things they wish but the vision holds.

Now, he had these visions, wrote down things, not because they were things that came out of his mind as such but it is as if he was spoken through. In a most amazing manner he had a sense that he was exposed to the very background of all existence, that he was in touch with the life out of which all things were evolved, all things were emanated, all things came, so that always whatever he saw, whatever he was doing he saw it both as the object at which he was looking, or the object that he was experiencing and he saw it as that behind all objects, behind all existences. And he wrote some of these things down and got into trouble. They began—there was a certain Lutheran minister who read this and he said, "This man is dangerous."[12] And he went before the town council and presented the case and Boehme was not even permitted to go home to tell his family goodbye. They just told him to keep on going outside the city. And he stayed out all night, nowhere to sleep and then one of the men happened to read one of the things and then when he read it, he thought, "Well, that's pretty good."[13] You see, he had been put out on the basis of the 'big lie,' that's all, on the basis of the big lie.[14] And he finally lost, however, because he was told not to write anymore but he hadn't written in the first place. It had written in him. It was like the little boy who whistled in class. The teacher said, "Johnny, did you whistle?" "No, I didn't whistle. It whistled itself." Well, that's the way he wrote, so when these mere men said to him under some ban of being exiled, "You must not write anymore." Then he wanted to be a good citizen. He wanted to stay with his family, and he said, "All right I'll do the best I can." And then he tried, but this tidal wave caught him and swept him out again and he could not help himself whatever may be the consequences. So long after he was exiled this man kept on saying these terrible things about him and then finally—to pull this story together to go on with this concept—when [Boehme] died, the prestige bearing members of the states, the princes, felt he'd have to be buried from the church. And at first, [his opponents] said, "No, you can't bury him from the church. You can't do that. It defames the house of God to have this child of light buried from it." And the minister who had been opposing him all these years also died, died I think before Boehme,[15] and his assistant—his successor being

---

12. Thurman is actually conflating to two accounts. First it was Gregorius Richter, the leading Lutheran pastor of Görlitz, Germany, who publicly denounced Boehme's first treatise, *Aurora* (originally titled "The Rising of the Dawn" (*Die Morgenroete im Aufgang*, 1612) as heretical. Second, Pastor Richter stirred greater controversy and with the town Council of Görlitz on March 26, 1624 exiled Boehme for his first published book, *The Way of Christ* (*Weg zu Christo*), which was released on New Year's Day, 1624.

13. The reference is to Dr. Benjamin Hinkleman, a physician, who provided asylum for Boehme after he left Goerlitz and went to Dresden, May 9, 1624.

14. The "Big Lie" is a term associated with Nazi propaganda, and the belief that the bigger and more brazen the lie, the more widely it will be believed.

15. Gregorious Richter died August 1624. Ironically the pastor's son with the assistance of the Dutch diplomat, Coenraad van Beuningen, collected and edited fragments of Boehme's works and published them in 1682.

true to his predecessor—wouldn't take his funeral.[16] As a matter of fact he got sick so that he could not make it.[17]

Now, he was persecuted, not because he was a bad man and not because he was a good man, but because he was a man who had an insight that was out of step with his time. That's all. The people who persecuted him were not bad people. No, they were good people. They were people who were doing the most natural thing in the world and that is, hold what you have because if you turn it loose you might not get anything else. And anybody who comes along to try to take it away from you, you better hold it. Now, that's the story in a nutshell.

Now, how did he deal with the problem that I set up in the early part of our thinking together. There were two wills, says Boehme, two wills. One will that goes out this way, goes out to man, to the world, to all aspects of life; and then there's a will that moves back toward the core. No man can understand, no man can understand anything in the world of phenomena, anything in the world of experience if all that he sees is what he is looking at. Now, if his knowledge is limited to that which is formal, discursive logic then he deals always with half truths. Reason, says he, is very important. But reason is very limited for it can only deal with the externals for the multiplication of externals. It cannot deal with the inner relatedness of these manifestations. So, the clue then is that the individual must, as he experiences and deals with particular things in the world about him, must deal with them not as if they were ends in themselves, but he must deal with them doubly. He must deal with them as they are seen by him as being at the moment of observation but at the same time he must see

---

16. Rufus Jones writes, "His old enemy, Richter, had died a few months before him, but the new pastor was of the same temper and refused to preach his funeral sermon. The second pastor of the city was finally ordered by the Governor of Lausitz to preach the sermon, which he began with the words, 'I had rather have walked a hundred and twenty miles than preach this sermon!'" *Spiritual Reformers*, 168.

17. On a rather ironic note, this episode parallels the difficulties Thurman's family had in finding a church and minister willing to bury his step-father, Saul Solomon Thurman, after his death in around 1908; see *Footprints of a Dream: The Story of the Fellowship Church for All Peoples* (New York: Harper and Brothers, 1959) 15–16; WHAH 4–6. And like Boehme, Saul Solomon Thurman's funeral sermon was preached by a minister hostile and unsympathetic to his step-father's life (though in the case of Saul Solomon Thurman, the cause of the problem was his lack of religiosity, rather than, for Boehme, what many perceived as his excessive and unusual piety).

in them that of which the particular expression is but one tiny aspect of, [and] ultimately hope that there will be in my life a moment when I shall see God face to face with nothing in between, not even my ego.

Now, when you apply this to ethics in human relations, then you get something very different for he says, "When I see a man" to put it into our language, "When I see a man I must apply to him," what Boehme calls, "creative imagination."[18] And he means by that the insight that comes from the way that the will moves back to its core and then from the core back out into the world looking at the world from within the experience of the center. That's what he is talking about.

Now, when I apply that to human beings a very interesting thing happens because when I see this man, I realize that he is a twig on a tree, a tree on which all of us are located. So that I see him both as John Jones, mean or not mean, beautiful or ugly, sick or well. That is the contextual point at which I relate to him, but all the time with this other dimension of my vision which he heartily calls the creative imagination and the exercise of this other will, I see him as the fullest, most complete manifestation of his life. So that when I see a sick person, I see him sick, I read his temperature, I understand all of that with one lens; with the other lens I see him well, whole, hale. And my ethical responsibility is to deal with him sick, limited from the [other] vantage point out here, [in which he is] whole, hale, complete. Do you see what he is saying? It is a tremendous thing—that I meet him here and see him there quite realistically and accurately calling everything I see by the name that is most accurate but at the same time the point at which I really relate to him is at this point out here. Now, Boehme says that I do that, I bring the sense of the whole to bear upon my relation to the man in the particular. So that I deal with you, to say this in ordinary language now, I deal with you where you are as

---

18. Kevin Fischer comments on how the creative imagination functions in both William Blake and Jacob Boehme: "abstract reasoning alone gives only a partial view, one that can distort and limit our understanding and the world that we do experience. By contrast, the creative embodied imagination places us more fully in existence, in ourselves and in the world; it makes possible true Reason; it reveals all the profound potential that is too often unexplored and unrealized in us; and by doing so it affords us a vital living understanding of and relationship with the Divine. Kevin Fischer, "William Blake and Jacob Boehme: Imagination, Experience and the Limitations of Reason," *Temenos Academy Review* 20 (2017): 2.

you are from within a meaning of you that is more than you are at that particular time.[19] And by dealing with you in that way I touch the core in you of which this thing out here that I see with my second vision is but a reflection and I stimulate it and it begins to grow and expand and take over so that before my very eyes again and again the miracle takes place that when, with this creative imagination the Boehme talks about, I bring to bear upon this individual the fullest reach of my sense of the whole, then with reference to him, to love as he calls it. Then before my very eyes I see a miracle take place in him. It is very interesting, isn't it, how all of the finest minds that are working in the field of psychotherapy are saying exactly that thing: that when they get through analyzing and understanding what is wrong in this personality, what is disturbed, they say if this sick mind could ever become aware that it is exposed to an enveloping whole love and in its response to that love it begins—the core begins to expand, blossom. And he's put his hands on a thing that we all feel in our own way, there is nobody in this room upstairs or downstairs who does not have somewhere lurking around in his spirit a hunger, a hunger to be completely and inclusively saluted, cared for, loved. And in the magic of that vitalism my spirit begins to stir, and as it stirs it sets up processes that wash me clean of my fears, of my insecurities, of all the things that choke my life. Boehme says that it is possible for one human

---

19. At a number of places Thurman speaks to the nature and role of the imagination in ways that affirm Boehme's notion of the *creative imagination*. For Thurman, "Imagination is a constituent part of the individual's nature as a spiritual being. Imagination can be used as a veritable messenger of spirit, when the individual through self-transcendence puts himself in another's place. Imagination, in this sense, is the pathway to empathy. Through the use of imagination, the individual is enabled to transcend himself and reach the other at the core of his being, at the seat of 'common consciousness.' In doing so, the other is addressed at a place beyond all blame and fault. This, according to Thurman, is the experience of compassion. When an individual is addressed at the centermost place of personality, she experiences a sense of wholeness and harmony. This is the 'common ground' of our relations with others." In his 1971 Hester Lectures at Golden Gate Baptist Seminary, Mill Valley, CA, Thurman says, "Imagination is the peculiar quality of mind that enables a man to stand in his own place, defined by the uniqueness of his life's story, and project himself into another person's life or situation. He makes soundings there, looking out upon life through the other's eyes, even as he remains himself. It is to inform one's self of the view from 'the other side.'" See Walter Earl Fluker, *Ethical Leadership: The Quest for Character, Civility and Community* (Minneapolis: Fortress Press, 2009), 72.

being to deal with another human being through this clumsy device that he uses, that Boehme uses—from one point of view clumsy—double vision, double view: seeing in time, in circumstance, in vicissitude but dealing with time, circumstance, vicissitude from a dimension outside of time, circumstance and vicissitude. An awkward and simple way to say it: to walk on the earth by the light in the sky. And what a difference it makes whenever it happens to us and how tremendous it must be to someone else when through us it happens to them.

THOMAS À KEMPIS

17 July 1953
Fellowship Church

This concluding sermon in the 1953 "Men Who Have Walked with God" series is about one of Thurman's favorite texts, but one, as he told the congregation, he had never spoken about in public before, Thomas à Kempis's (ca. 1380–1471) The Imitation of Christ, *probably the most popular Christian devotional book ever written.[1] Thurman, without drawing exact parallels to postwar America, saw Kempis responding to the situation in fifteenth-century Europe, which Thurman saw as a time when old and dead structures held sway, long after whatever utility they had once enjoyed was past, giving the example of oak trees on which the dead leaves stay on their branches until spring, when "very quietly what all of the organized violence of winter was unable to do the quiet pushing of the sap inside the tree accomplishes."*

Despite the fact that there were many "things in it that are not a part of our thinking or not a part of our own outlook," such as the book's praise of "humble subjection under the government of a superior," Thurman thought The Imitation of Christ *was a "great book."*

---

1. Thomas à Kempis (ca. 1380–1471) was born Thomas Hermerken in the Rhineland town of Kempen near Düsseldorf (now in Germany.) In the mid-1390s he relocated to Deventer and became involved in the Brethren of the Common Life, a pietist, semi-monastic movement of popular spirituality, centered in what is now the Netherlands. The Brethren of the Common Life gave birth to the *devotio moderna*, a movement committed to a spirituality that gave priority to education, service to the poor, moderation, imitation of the virtues of Christ, disciplined meditation, solitude, and silence. Kempis took minor orders in 1408 and was ordained in 1413. He spent much of his long life at the Augustinian monastery at Greenburg, near Zwolle, Netherlands. Although Kempis is credited with writing a number of works, the most celebrated by far is *The Imitation of Christ*, a small book written in Latin between 1418 and 1427. First printed ca. 1471, by the end of the fifteenth century it had been printed in Latin and in various vernacular translations over one hundred times.

Thurman praises the monastic voice of *The Imitation of Christ, and the importance of stillness and quiet in religious contemplation. and what could be accomplished without bombast.* As an illustration, Thurman recalls an experience with a student who regularly visited his office for several days and with few exceptions sat in silence, avoiding mundane conversation. Kempis avoids reducing life's conflicts to stark dualities. Rather, in Thurman's words, Kempis points out that "much of the confusion of my life is rooted in the fact that again and again I must wrestle with issues that are not clearly defined."

This was not only the final sermon in the 1953 Men Who Walked with God series. It was also likely the final sermon Thurman would deliver as minister of Fellowship Church. About two months after this sermon was delivered, he was preaching his initial sermon as dean of chapel of Boston University. The sermon obliquely spoke to the fact that many in the church looked to Thurman as an unimpeachable source of spiritual authority and were bereft at the prospect of his leaving. "So if we don't have courage, if we are unwilling to go through the discipline necessary to awaken within us the authority that we must have to be free, then our only alternative is to seek refuge in some symbol of authority, be it the church, be it the book, be it your mother or your father or the psychiatrist." To make the point in a different way, he paraphrases Virgil's farewell to Dante as he moves to a realm he cannot enter: *This is as far as we can go—as far as I can go. From now on you are on your own.*

Continuing our series, I would like to do something I have never attempted to do in public before. I'd like to think for a little while about the great classic that has perhaps had a greater influence on the mind and the thinking of our immediate and remote background in America and in the Western world than any other book perhaps except the Bible, and that is Thomas à Kempis's *The Imitation of Christ*.

At the very beginning of my own ministry, one morning when I had returned from Cleveland, as I walked into the house the doorbell was ringing—the telephone, I mean, was ringing—and when I answered, it was a man with great tremor in his voice asking me if I would come over to his home immediately.² It was about quarter to seven in the morning. I got my bicycle and went over there. He met me—his little boy met me at the door and took me upstairs and he said, "Mother and Dad are in the room." And I went into this bedroom and there I saw this lady, a member of the church and friend. She had gone to sleep the night before and in her sleep she had a stroke, and when she awoke the next morning she awoke paralyzed. And the shock was so tremendous that one could see literally her mind slipping out of its socket and then—I sat on the bed and I held the hand that was not paralyzed with my right hand and with my left hand I thumbed through various pages of *The Imitation of Christ*, reading at random and then being quiet, reading some more and then being quiet. That went on from ten minutes to seven in the morning when I got there until 2:30 in the afternoon. And at 2:30 all the raving was over and she dropped into a deep sleep.

The Imitation of Christ. Many people are frightened by the title because to them it is—the title suggests something with which they do not wish to have anything to do. But it is a great book despite all of the things in it that are not a part of our thinking or not a part of our own outlook, are not a part of the materials that are meaningful to us. Yet there is a great body of richness and vitality and meaning that has almost no counterpart in our literature.

Now, I'd like to feel my way through it just a little. There is a great deal of confusion, of course, about who the author is. That's a part of being respectable. I guess that there is confusion about Shakespeare and somebody else, Bacon, I believe they say.³ They don't know whether Thomas à Kempis was Thomas à Kempis or whether anybody else was Thomas à Kempis and somebody else wrote it. Well, that's a very wonderful exercise

---

2. Thurman's first position after graduating from Rochester Theological Seminary in 1926 was at the Mt. Zion Baptist Church in Oberlin, Ohio.

3. Most scholars accept Thomas à Kempis as the main author of *The Imitation of Christ,* although some argue for a more collaborative authorship. As for Thurman's mention of the argument that Francis Bacon (1561–1621) or some other person other than the William Shakespeare who was born in Stratford-on-Avon in 1564 was the author of the thirty-six plays contained in the *First Folio* (published in 1623) and other works usually attributed to Shakespeare, the evidence is non-existent, despite industrious efforts to the contrary.

for people who are concerned about the jot and the tittle. But it has nothing to do with the insight.

There was a period, the fourteenth and fifteenth centuries, a period when it seemed as if in one sense all the lights were going out and in another sense they were being born.[4] It's like a certain kind of oak tree. In the fall all of the life goes out of the leaves, and then they turn golden and then they turn brown and a kind of stale brown. And they remain stale brown all the winter. The winds can't break them away; the hail doesn't seem or sleet doesn't seem to be able to pull these leaves away from the branches. They stick it out defying the storm and the winter. And then the springtime comes. And when the springtime comes, very quietly what all of the organized violence of winter was unable to do the quiet pushing of the sap inside the tree accomplishes. And these leaves fall off because the tree now turns away from the business of clinging onto the leaves that are old and dead and gives itself to the business of creating new leaves, and in the creating of the new leaves the old leaves drop off.

I think sometimes civilizations and cultures are like that. I think so, and such a period was the period when *The Imitation of Christ* was written. There were rumblings all around, rumblings of despair and rumblings of optimism. The sons of France had had a hard time. They had lost their faith and their confidence, and then a girl, a girl who heard the wind whispering in the mulberry trees and the sound of which became to her many-tongued voices that broke into her spirit and laid hold upon the movement of her mind, and Joan of Arc[5] swept out to redeem her people. That was the period. Columbus was dreaming about new worlds. "It's madness to sail an ocean that had never been sailed before. It's madness to look for land the existence of which is a question." "If Columbus had reflected thus, he would never have weighed anchor, but with that madness he discovered a new world. That was the climate, the climate. The

---

4. Thurman's argument about the decadence of later medieval culture closely follows the argument of the Dutch historian Johan Huizinga's (1872–1945) well-known book, *The Waning of the Middle Ages* (London: E. Arnold, 1924), first published in Dutch in 1919.

5. For Thurman on Joan of Arc, see "Man and the Moral Struggle: St. Joan," 27 November 1949, published in *Moral Struggle and the Prophets,* volume 1 of *Walking with God: The Sermon Series of Howard Thurman* (ed. Peter Eisenstadt and Walter E. Fluker; Maryknoll, NY: Orbis Books, 2020), 74–84.

church was in difficulties just now, and there were men who had withdrawn more and more from the traffic of life, from all of the struggle and who felt that they could only find peace by withdrawing.

I remember, I think I have mentioned this to you once, years ago I was at a student conference down in the southern part of Missouri, and there were students who came from Mississippi and Texas and Oklahoma, etc., and I had appointments in the afternoon from two to five. Well, I noticed when I got my list that one person from Lubbock, Texas A&M college[6] down there had signed up the hour from two to three every one of the days that I was there. I wondered, "What does that mean?" So the first day at two o'clock he came, tall, lanky fellow with the neophyte's vision of a cowboy. He sat on the floor with his back against the wall, lighted his cob pipe and then introduced himself, giving me his name, asking me my name and then he sat. For one hour he sat and not a word did he say. At the end of the hour he got up, and he thanked me for the time, and said, "I'll be back tomorrow at two o'clock." The next day at two o'clock he came and sat. Nothing was said; and the next day he came, and in the middle of the third day, the third hour, some young woman came riding into the grounds on an Arabian horse—that is he said it was an Arabian horse—and he looked at me and he looked out at her and the horse and he said, "What a tragic thing it is to keep any kind of animal, human or otherwise, in a situation in which that animal can't be happy." That was all he said that day. And then the last day he came and he got up to leave at fifteen minutes before three. And he thanked me for—he said, "I thank you very much for these four hours of communion we have had together. It is a wonderful thing," he said, "To sit together in an atmosphere that is not full of pro-ing and con-ing." He said, "Give my love to all your people and I will give your love to all my people."[7] And he shook my hand and disappeared. We all feel like pulling away from the atmosphere of pro-ing

---

6. Texas A&M University is in College Station, not Lubbock.

7. Thurman does not mention that the student from Texas A&M was white, perhaps because he thought in 1953 it would be obvious, and when he told Thurman, "Give my love to all your people and I will give your love to all my people," the student likely wanted to spend time with a black person as an equal, without having to defend himself, or asking his counterpart to defend himself.

and con-ing, whether it is in terms of the traffic of life or whether it is in terms merely of the tensions by which we are surrounded.

We see reflected in *The Imitation of Christ* stark wrestling with an interesting kind of dualism, not merely, or not in essence, the dualism between darkness and light, between evil and that which is good; not the fundamental or metaphysical struggle of the human spirit as it wrestles for some kind of integration, some kind of completed light, not that so much; but the struggle in the *Imitation* is the struggle between the world with all the things in it, the good things and the bad things. The struggle between the world, the details of living, the responsibilities of experience, those things or that thing, and the spirit of God. Now, from our point of view it may be a phony struggle, but when we see what this man does with it then we can relate to it in terms of our own struggle because the struggle that he defines is a universal one. Stating it in an almost exaggerated manner, it would take a shape like this in our minds, in my mind, anyway. It is easy enough to take sides when the battle is clearly drawn between good and evil. Very often it is easy enough to take a position for right when the opposite position is clearly and accurately defined, but much of the confusion of my life is rooted in the fact that again and again I must wrestle with issues that are not clearly defined. Here are two things which commend themselves in terms of a total sense of goodness, but one somehow seems to me to have a quality that the other lacks. And I must make up my mind between two good things, not between two things, one of which is evil and one is good. That is what he is getting at, that we are in the world, we are involved in the world, but his answer is to withdraw. So his word in *The Imitation* is the classic and creative expression of the very genius of the monastic movement in Western civilization, in Western culture particularly in Christian faith.

Now, one comment about that, and then two other things that I want to say and I won't keep you much longer. There is something to be said for the—how to say it?—there is something to be said for the tendency that emerges in human history that seems to exaggerate some particular virtue and throw it all out of line with anything that is normal and natural because it was in the monastery with its insistence on celibacy and all the other things that went with it, that it was possible for a new kind of reverence growing basically out of the distilled essence of a distortion, a new kind of reverence to invade the common life. And that is important to remember; I won't explore it further but it is important to remember.

Now, in *The Imitation* there is a recognition of the place of authority. And I wrote a sentence down, if I can put my hands on it. This is the key sentence: "Go whither thou wilt; thou shall find no rest but in humble subjection under the government of a superior. Many have discovered themselves imagining to find happiness in change. Go where thou wilt, thou shall find no rest but in humble subjection under the government of a superior."[8] Do you believe that? There is something in us that always wants to be bound. There is something deep within us that wants to surrender to some kind of control. There is something deep within us that always wants to relate to something that is fixed, unchanging, permanent, solid, substantial, something that wants authority even as there is something deep within us that is always in rebellion against authority. And what the monastic movement provided, as expressed through the wonderful pages of *The Imitation*, was the source of authority, of changelessness through which the individual, lost in the traffic of the world of his time, could relate and feel that at least under its shelter he will find strength and protection and stability.

Now, put over against that another line I'd like to read from almost a contemporary. This is the way [Dante][9] puts the same thing in another dimension. You remember after Virgil takes him to a certain point, he has been under the domination of authority and control all along, and finally he arrives at a point where Virgil says, "This is as far as we can go—as far as I can go. From now on you are on your own. Expect no more sanction of warning voice or sign from me. Free of thy abridgement to choose discrete, judicious. To distrust thy sense were henceforth error." Up to this time to trust your sense was error, now from this point on to distrust thy

---

8. "It is a great matter to live in obedience, to be under a superior, and not to be at our own disposing. It is much safer to obey, than to govern. Many live under obedience, rather for necessity than for charity; such are discontented, and do easily repine. Neither can they attain to freedom of mind, unless they willingly and heartily put themselves under obedience for the love of God. Go whither you will, you shall find no rest, but in humble subjection under the government of a superior. The imagination and change of places have deceived many" (*Imitation of Christ,* chapter IX, "Of Obedience and Subjection" [CreateSpace Independent Publishing Platform, 2015], 10).

9. Dante Alighieri (1265–1321), Italian poet and author of the *Divine Comedy.*

sense [would] henceforth [be an] error. "I invest thee then with crown and mitre sovereign over thyself." [10] Now there is the issue defined and that is where we are caught always. And what the discipline, the sense of stability, the sense of emotional security that comes from relating ourselves to something that doesn't change, the feeling that at last I am not ultimately responsible for my life. "Oh, Thou who changest not, abide with me." There is that sense, and there is the other: that there shall be no freedom ultimately until the authority to which the individual relates, the authority under the shadow of which the individual finds his emotional stability, is an authority that he discovers deep within himself. And that's the paradox. So if we don't have courage, if we are unwilling to go through the discipline necessary to awaken within us the authority that we must have to be free, then our only alternative is to seek refuge in some symbol of authority, be it the church, be it the book, be it your mother or your father or the psychiatrist. But the whole business of the relationship of any authority that we need at some stage in our lives is so to work and knead the personalities of our material until at last there emerges out of the essence of the ebb and flow of one's own vitality and being the authority. The mystic says that doesn't happen until at last the man discovers that the source of the authority that is deep within him is the God that is in him. And when he relates to that then he has found the peace that passeth all understanding.

Now, I will stop, but I am not through. *The Imitation of Christ* gave very practical advice, practical suggestions; and it is in this area that I found his book most useful, over and over again. For instance, he says one little thing—then I really will stop—he says that when you go to bed at night cast up your accounts, you know. That may not be a good accounting word, but balance your books. When you go to bed at night get your books straight, look back over the day, get it straight. Then when you wake up in the morning, wake up with some sort of plan for your

---

10. Virgil tells Dante, "No longer expect word or sign from me. Free, upright, and whole is thy will and it were a fault not to act on its biddings. Therefore over thyself I crown and mitre thee" (*The Divine Comedy of Dante Alighieri: Purgatorio* [trans. John D. Sinclair; Oxford: Oxford University Press, 1939], 357). These are Virgil's last words to Dante in the *Divine Comedy*. Thurman is quoting from an 1847 translation of the *Purgatorio* by Henry Francis Cary.

day, for your life for that day. It need not be a great elaborate dramatic something, but some plan that will guide you through the day when you don't have time to stop to make up your mind, but you are tarrying in the bed early in the morning for a minute or two, or ten minutes, so get it charted. And then he said, don't ever let yourself get too idle. He said that's not good. Then he says further, find some way by which you can share whatever there is that is precious to you with somebody else so that in your joy you will not be alone even as in your sorrow.

Now he has much to say about the cross, what it means and about the meaning of the sacrament of communion. But one word about the cross. That wherever a man deals with the responsibilities and the burdens and the tragedies of his life, there he is reproducing in some measure the experience that is for him a redemptive one. Therefore, said he, "shun not"—strange words for one living in a monastery—"shun not the encounter with pain, for the encounter with pain opens up the way to redemption."[11] And I am grateful to God that *The Imitation* came my way when I was still a young man and has not deserted me through the years. And if you don't have a copy, I hope that someday you will get a copy.

---

11. *Imitation*, book II, chapter XII, "On the Necessity of Bearing the Cross."

Additional Sermons and Lectures

The Religion of the Inner Life

ca. 1950
Fellowship Church, San Francisco

This sermon was probably delivered in 1950, in conjunction with the first "Men Who Have Walked with God" series, which Thurman gave at Fellowship Church from late 1949 through mid-1950.[1] In the sermon, Thurman first considers the relationship between science and religion. He writes that the scope of religion has contracted as the sphere of science has expanded. When he was a young boy, he worshiped an external God and expected that God to help him with his tasks, such as solving quadratic equations. He later discovered that what he had thought was God answering his prayers was only the firing of his "neurons." Thurman suggests that there is a complementary relationship between science and religion, in which science seeks to answer the question, "How?" But beyond the limits of this question, the scientific method is unable to provide an adequate response to the most fundamental question of the human spirit, "Why?" The mystic's quest for knowledge, Thurman claims, goes beyond the restricted boundaries of empirical investigation and rational ordering of the world; rather, the mystic is in search of an aspect of human experience that is simultaneously "an element, an aspect, a quality that is God in man."

Thurman then reckons with the phenomenon of identity as a starting point of the exploration of mysticism, which he felt was "the fundamental crux of all that the human spirit means by religious experience." The goal

---

1. The typescript of "Religion and the Inner Life" has, in Thurman's handwriting, "Mystical Religion" and "Men Who Have Walked with God, Part I" crossed out above the title "'The Religion and the Inner Life." If this sermon was delivered as an introduction to the first "Men Who Have Walked with God" series, it would have probably been delivered in 1949.

is to make one's awareness the centering point of the quest for self-transcendence, which is found in the core or "divine spark" of existence. This centering point is beyond all doctrines, institutions, religious rituals, or practices because it is already resident within the individual. It is the individual's job to activate this process through awareness. It is then, Thurman suggests, that one begins to "live." He identifies four ways that are part of the work of becoming alive. One is the stimulus response of a certain feeling, impulse, in contact with another that includes moral initiative as in "put[ting] a dime in a beggar's cup." A second has to do with a gradual opening or realization of the path that is beckoning toward an inner experience of which one is conscious but not fully aware. The third stimulus response is external but calls to something within the individual. Thurman claims that this experience is analogous to viewing a majestic mountain range. He wonders if there is something of the magnitude in the mountain range (the mystic's object of consciousness) that sheds light on the magnificence of the same quality of experience within. Finally, there is the stimulus response that is coterminous with the quest for a "new life," as in the conversion experience of George Fox.[2] For the mystic, Thurman says, this experience of becoming a new creature is a bit different from the traditional language of "being born again." It is rather the response to this stimulus, disclosed in a new center out of which the mystic moves and "increasingly all the details of the life are more and more organized."

In addition, Thurman identifies here, as in other places, key terms of the mystical encounter such as detachment, illumination, discipline, the last being the dynamic push and pull of the mystic's struggle to return to the center that calls to the integrity of his/her inner experience, the pursuit that has to do with the moral quality of the will.

---

2. George Fox (1624–1691), the founder of the Quakers, describes his enlightening experience of union in this manner, experienced at Pendle Hill in East Lancaster, England, in 1652: "Now I was come up in the spirit through the Flaming Sword, into the Paradise of God. All things were new; and all the creation gave unto me another smell than before, beyond what words can utter. I knew nothing but pureness, and innocency, and righteousness; being renewed into the image of God by Christ Jesus, to the state of Adam, which he was in before he fell. The creation was opened to me, and it was showed me how all things had their names given them according to their nature and virtue" (George Fox, *Journal of George Fox* [Richmond, IN: Friends United Press, 1983], 97).

I want you to work with me on the fundamental proposition that mystical religion, or the religion of the inner life, is at long last the fundamental crux of all that the human spirit means by religious experience. We are scarcely aware of the fact that modern science has made radical inroads upon all of the areas of religious meaning and value by dispelling in one way or another vast hulks of the mysterious in life. They have said that the Earth is not the center of everything as we thought; that the Earth is but a tiny speck of stardust whirling mathematically through space. There are millions and millions of suns and stars and universes, and this little thing we call our sun is just one little justice-of-the-peace guarding one little segment, while the great court extends on and on.

The psychologists have been working on us. In my childhood I prayed "Now I lay me down to sleep" and the Lord's Prayer every morning and evening all through the grades and through high school until I hit simultaneous quadratics, and then I began tacking on a little footnote to my prayer, asking God in addition to take some special consideration of the fact that I had no inclination or interest in mathematics but I had to pass. I would add a little magic by putting my algebra under my pillow because the general superstition was that it would get into my head during the night. When I went to college and began studying psychology, I found out what happened, that technical things called neurons had worked away at a pattern that I had established. To me at that time it had been an answer to prayer, but when later I studied psychology, I had all of this [as an] explanation.

Is there any area left, is there any sense in which we may continue to experience the meaning of religion stripped bare of all of the things that have been taken away from us as the result of science? Science does not try to answer the most crucial question that we want to know about, and that question is, "Why?" Science undertakes to answer the question "How," not "Why," and therefore science is almost always descriptive in its character rather than explanatory. The human spirit is so imbued with hero worship and a quaint kind of adoration that we constantly urge the scientist to get out of his little area and tell us all about everything else. He is just a human being, and he tries to do it—and we move from chaos to chaos. As long as the scientist is operating in the narrow context which he sets up for himself, he makes an important and significant contribution to the understanding of certain aspects of our life. But there are moods of the human spirit which cannot be envisioned or felt or sensed or analyzed by the methodology of the scientist, whatever his claims may be.

Now the mystic insists that in every human being, in addition to all that he is able to grasp with his mind, there is an element, an aspect, a quality, that is God in the man.

Have you ever tried to explain yourself to someone? You used all the words you knew, every analogy that you could get your hands on, every device by which you could reduce *you* to a manageable unit of communication. What happens always? Even with the person who loves you most deeply, who understands you most profoundly and most intimately—always there is something left over in you that is not quite able to get said.

Now the mystic insists that this core, this nucleus, this uncreated element,[3] this essence, is the link that each living thing has with the ground and the creator of all of life; and the goal of the striving of the individual is to make this awareness become for him the clue for all that he means by life and all that he is trying to experience in life. The mystic says that there is in every human being this spark which is God; that it may be covered over by all sorts of things incident to the limitations or difficulties to which the body is heir, or due to accidents or aberrations that affect the possibility of unfolding or flowering, but it is always there because it cannot die. Whenever I become aware of it, I begin to live.

The [claim?] of the mystic is, at last, that you don't need anything to bring you to God. You don't need a mediator. You don't need an institution. You don't need a ceremony or a ritual. God is in me, and the ladder from the earth to sky is [available?]. So, I can ascend my own altar stairs wherever I am, under any circumstances, and the key to the understanding of the experience, and to the experience itself, is never in the hands of any other human being.

---

3. A term associated with Meister Eckhart.

When I love people, then I find God in me. Whether I bow my knee at any altar doesn't make any difference, the God in me begins to move up through the corridors of my mind and my emotions giving them a kind of glory, an aura; and moves out from me and broods over you; and there moves in you the same quality until it begins to start from way down and begins to mount up and up and up until at last it fulfills itself. If you love somebody, you never give that person up. Isn't it interesting how Jesus always insisted upon this, and how completely we have missed it in our doctrine? Nothing that I can do can kill the God in me. Nothing. *Nothing.* Since I can't destroy it, perhaps if I listen, if I can become still enough, I will hear it whisper to me the precise word I need to take away so much of my unhappiness and my misery and my pessimism about the nature of life and the meaning of my own life. If I can be still so that the God in me can get on the march, I don't need any priest, I don't need any preacher, I don't even need any church. All these will help perhaps, but I don't need them. At last God is in me, and if I find him in me, when I come to church, I'll find him in the church. The burden of proof at last is on the vitality of my own awareness.

There are three or four different kinds of stimuli to which we respond, stimuli which indicate something to us about our inner lives. There is the response to a sudden stimulus, an impulse to put a dime into a beggar's hat. It comes quickly, before you have time to think about a social agency; that moment just before you think "I can't contribute to pandering and panhandling. Maybe he is going to take it and buy some whiskey." It is that little moment that comes just before—as some would say—before your senses take over. Now what happens in that stimulus-response moment? Something suddenly appears inside of you that gives you a new center. It may not last but a minute. It is a new point of orientation, a new sense that makes you pass a swift and sometimes a devastating judgment upon everything else that you were doing before that moment came upon you.

Then there is the stimulus that comes so gradually that you don't know when it started, but little by little you begin to realize that you are looking at things differently. You don't know at what point the thing took place, at what point you got on this road, but as you think about it you realize that it has been going on a long time, although you were not aware of it. That kind of stimulus discloses areas of meaning inside of you of which you were conscious but of which you were not aware—and often there is a distinction between the two.

There is a stimulus that comes from the outside and something inside of you rises to meet it. In talking to the children this morning I told them about the experience I had in seeing the great mountain range, in the northern part of India; how suddenly in the darkness there was a faint glow, and then by magic what was all blackness became all glory, because the sunlight burst on this range of white snow peaks while all below remained in darkness.[4]

Something within me stirred and lifted itself to salute that moment. I don't know whether it was the breaking of the light on [the mountain range?] that inspired this thing in me, creating it from the outside and putting it inside of me; or whether there was something of that magnitude already in me which came to attention when there was something of comparable magnitude outside of me that called it.

A kind of stimulus comes as a result of the work on the part of the individual to discover within himself a new self. Have you ever had that experience, when something made of you a new creature? Though perhaps you didn't last long as a new creature. George Fox says that when the Light broke in him after so long a question, he had his tremendous vision on Pendle Hill, he came up "past the angel with the flaming sword and all the world had a new smell." A new self emerges and that new self becomes the center of the orientation of my life. Love does that for us, for it inspires in an individual what was a sleeping, relaxed sense of worth and value and meaning, and when this slumbering thing awakens, the kind of radiance that it circulates through all the corridors of one's life makes the individual see in himself what he had never seen before. This, which mystics are always talking about, is a little more than what is traditionally regarded as conversion. It is the discovery of a new

---

4. Thurman is referring to his experience of viewing the sunrise over Mt. Everest during the Christmas holidays in northern India in 1935. "At first there was just a faint finger of pink in the sky, then suddenly the whole landscape burst into one burnished gold radiance: everything was clear. Beyond the solitary glowing peak of Everest rose" (WHAH, 127).

center around which increasingly all of the details of the life are more and more organized.

The other way to say it is that it is the discovery of the God that is already in you. That is the way the mystic puts it; and his lifelong pursuit is to ride in the area of this consciousness, to keep pushing the frontier back so that more and more of this new sense of the inner presence and vitality of God will free all the space of his life. That is what he is insisting upon all of the time; therefore, it is against that background that we must understand some of the language that he uses.

"Detachment" is one of the great words of the mystic. Detachment is—detachment! We do it all the time, don't we? If we didn't, we couldn't survive. Since you have been sitting there you have detached yourself from what is going on, and put your mind into yesterday, into last week, into what you are going to do this afternoon. Every now and then you check back into the stream of what I am saying! But the difficulty is that we become detached most often without reference to a center. We do it randomly, but the mystic is [concerned] about doing it with reference to the center, with reference to this new awareness of the consciousness of God in him. A new kind of value judgement appears so that everything that he does and everything in which he shares at last has to be interpreted by him in the light of its bearing on this central attachment. His detachment from things is in essence an attachment to the disclosure of the Presence of God which he is sure is operative within him.

Another word mystics use is "illumination." Have you ever tried to explain something to someone when the person did not understand? You thought a minute and said it in another way, but the person did not understand. Then you remembered something about that person and explained in terms of something with which you knew he was familiar. The person looked at you and said, "Oh, I see." Then it was as if that person and this insight alone existed in all the universe. You didn't exist. Your explanation didn't exist. Nothing existed but the awareness in that moment of an idea, of a truth, that had had no existence up to that awareness. In its simplest terms that is what illumination is. It is more than a mental process. When Tolstoy saw a man get his head cut off at the guillotine in Paris, he said, "I know with all of myself, not just my mind, that capital punishment was wrong."[5] That is illumination, the moment when the light breaks, when the truth is clear.

One other word is "discipline." There is a curious sense of struggle resident in all living manifestations. There seems to be struggle at levels that reach far out beyond the mind and its operation. Every man knows what struggle is inside of his own heart. There are moments when I see that which calls me with clarity and conviction and urgency and insistence, and I recognize its validity and its priority with all the powers of my being, and even as I recognize it there is a stirring in me that pulls me in the other direction. We all know what that is if we are honest. Somehow I feel that if I can ever get the [clue] to the struggle that goes on inside of me, if I can ever get the low-down on my own inner battle, then I can be free, and I want to be free to follow with utter abandonment and a kind of riotous enthusiasm the light that breaks on my horizon, that always calls and beckons to me. But I have some accounts to settle first.

The mystic recognizes within himself that this is going on, and he identifies these things that work against the Light as being resident in the flesh, in the time-space involvement of his personality. If, somehow, he can reduce the body, reduce the sense awareness to a vanishing quantity, then automatically his spirit will be released to the Spirit. He believes it is possible to reduce the sense experience to manageable units of control if not to wipe them out. Eckhart says, "If I can empty myself of creatureliness, the God will have to fill me up."

The assumption is that there is a relationship between the discipline itself and the presence of God. If a man can understand the spiritual exercises and can give himself to contemplation and meditation and contrition and purging of his own heart, then automatically he will become in fuller and more complete possession of the living spirit of the living God. But it doesn't happen that way. No mystic claims finally that if you follow all the spiritual exercises you will get the illumination. But he says you can't get anywhere without them.

The mystic says, "My responsibility will be to work on the discipline. I don't know what God thinks, but I know that every time I look around, I'm in my own way. I don't need the wisdom of a great benevolent benign

---

5. See "Men Who Have Walked with God: Jane Steger," published in the current volume.

God to sit in judgment on the limitations that are inherent in my behavior, so I shall work at myself. I shall hack away at my limitations with honesty, with integrity, and if by chance the pruning of my tree causes His fruit to grow, how wonderful it will be; if not, I shall see the travail of my soul and be satisfied." So, the mystic rests his case at last on the integrity of his inner experience, which inner experience is to him the Light, the Truth, and the Way. Who can say he is wrong?

Mysticism and Social Change: God as Presence

12 July 1978
Pacific School of Religion

Howard Thurman, in his late seventies, was still teaching college students. One of the last courses he taught was in the summer of 1978, at the Pacific School of Religion, on one of his favorite subjects, "Mysticism and Social Change." Whether or not he planned this, the course has the feel of a valediction, a bringing together of his lifelong investigation and immersion in "the stream of the mystic's experience." Thurman's course consisted of fourteen lectures, and they were recorded. The lectures have a different quality from the sermons. They are more than twice as long as a typical sermon and are more meandering, with Thurman following sometime tangential trains of thought. (It is worth remembering as well that these lectures were delivered by a seventy-eight-year-old man.) The editors have selected two of these lectures for publication. This lecture covered many subjects: the nature of the mystic's experience, the connection between sin and suffering, his encounters with ghosts during his Florida childhood, his summer of military training at Howard University during World War I, watching a baseball game, and his moving re-creation of the final moments of Jesus on the cross.

Probably the most significant part of the lecture is his discussion of his understanding of God. "When I refer to God," he states, "I am not talking about a thing, I am not talking about an object: I am talking about a Presence." Thurman offers a description of his God; the Creator of Life, the "living stuff" out of which every living thing is fashioned, and the Life that exists outside of its particular manifestations, so that, as he says "God bottoms existence—bottoms it—bottoms it!" And when a mystic clears away all the personal detritus that usually blocks our awareness of this, through the tools of detachment, prayer, and meditation a connection is made to a reality that can only be described as "for instances," through a series of inadequate analogies. Thurman goes to great length to discuss these disciplines that provide occasions for coming home to oneself and discovering that God is also part of "the borning process," that is, God is longing to become "self-conscious."[1]

Golden it is, altogether golden whenever and wherever it is, that moment in which any man's soul moves to recover its *accord with God*. Golden it is if only because of all moments in a man's day. It indeed does mean most genuine and rewarding wealth to him. All that mankind agrees upon as being most worth living will come out of such moments.

> Occurring and recurring
> in the noisy house of the driven day,
> or in the quiet night,
> as one runs, or walks, or stands or sits,
> this moment
> of all moments known to human life,
> is the moment most gilded by life's rising sun,
> the moment in which the human spirit uplifts
> itself inquiring after unity with God.

Is it so that to be strong at the circumference a man must be strong at the center; that if one is poisoned at the center or weak or at war there he will hardly find peace, strength, or pleasantness at the circumference; that

---

1. This "search in common consciousness" as the realization of God coming to Godself is a recurring theme in Thurman. See HT, *The Search for Common Ground: An Inquiry into the Basis of Man's Experience of Community* (Richmond, IN: Friends United Press, 1986 [1st ed., 1971]); HT, *The Creative Encounter: An Interpretation of Religion and the Social Witness* (Richmond, IN: Friends United Press, 1972 [1st ed., 1954]), 37–38; HT, "The Great Hunger," published in volume 1 of this series, *Walking with God*; Mozella Gordon Mitchell, *Spiritual Dynamics of Howard Thurman's Theology* (Bristol, IN: Wyndham Hall Press, 1985), 52. See also Luther Smith, "Black Theology and Religious Experience," *Journal of the Interdenominational Theological Center* 7, no. 1 (Fall 1980): 59–72; and Henry J. Young, *Hope in Process: A Theology of Social Pluralism* (Minneapolis: Fortress Press, 1991).

he may masquerade and keep up appearances but he himself will deeply know that in business and in play, in all life's occupations and relations, in his points of view and in his emotional reactions to people and things and events things are wrong? Is all this so when a man is weak at his center?

> Then return unto thy rest,
> oh my soul!
> and leave and the wakening war of thy fragments
> for the wholeness that is in God.
> Said he not, "Be ye whole for I am whole"?
> Is it not written "Ye are complete in Him"?
> Lift up thy thought therefore,
> oh my soul,
> to Him who is thy central, primary,
> health and vigor.
> And bring thyself again, with intelligence and
> [with] will
> into conscious and confident accord with him.
> There rest thee
> and be strong.[2]

. . .

Two men faced each other in a prison cell. They belonged to different countries, their roots watered by streams from different cultures. One was under sentence of death, scheduled to be executed within a few short hours. The other was a visitor and friend, this even though months before they had been enemies in the Great War. They bade each other farewell for the last time. The visitor was deeply troubled, but he could not find his way through the emotional maze in which he was caught to give voice to what cried out for utterance. This is what he wanted to say but could not.

We may not be able to stop and undo the hard old wrongs of the great world outside. But through you and me no evil shall come either in the unknown where you are going or in this imperfect and haunted dimension of awareness through which I move. Thus between us we shall cancel

---

2. The sermon until this point is quoting Oswald McCall, *The Hand of God* (1939; repr. and expanded ed.; New York: Harper & Brothers, 1957), 139–40. For Thurman on McCall, see "Oswald McCall," in PHWT 5: 245–49.

out all private and personal evil; thus arrest private and personal consequences to blind action and reaction; thus prevent specifically the general incomprehension and misunderstanding, hatred and revenge of our time from spreading further. [I will come back to that paragraph many times before we are through so don't bother about it now.]

The forces at work in the world that seem to determine the future and the fate of mankind seem so vast, so impersonal and unresponsive to the will and desire of any individual that it is easy to abandon all hope for a sane and peaceful order of life for mankind. Nevertheless it is urgent to hold steadily in mind the utter responsibility of the solitary individual to do everything with all his heart and mind to arrest the development of the consequence of private and personal evil resulting from the interaction of the impersonal forces that surround us. To cancel out between you and another all personal and private evil, to put your life squarely on the side of the good thing because it is good and for no other reason is to anticipate the kingdom of God at the level of your own functioning.

At long last a man must be deeply convinced that the contradictions of life which he encounters are not final, that the radical tension between good and evil as he sees it and feels it does not have the last word about the meaning of life and the nature of existence; that there is a spirit in man and in the world working always against the thing that destroys and cuts down. Thus he will live wisely and courageously his little life. And those who see the sunlight in his face will drop their tools and follow him. There is no ultimate negation for the man for whom it is categorical that the ultimate destiny of man on this planet is a good destiny.[3] We will come back to that again and again and again.

I want to begin—you see, we are still working on meditation, bear that in mind—I mean on meditation as I see it, you know, which is not—which doesn't have anything to do with meditation as you see it—of necessity, I mean. We may be—we are talking about the same thing but there may be a desert and a sea between what I am saying and what you are thinking. But it's all right. I'm responsible for what I am saying.

It is important in the process of clearing the way, of detaching myself from the things that cloy and divert my spirit from the integrity of the

---

3. This is the end of the second reading, "No Contradictions Are Final," from HT, *The Inward Journey* (New York: Harper & Row, 1961), 105–6.

search and the quest. And one of the most critical ones is my own sense of guilt and personal limitations which I designate as sin. One of the serious handicaps, roadblocks—that's the word I want—to a sense of coming home to your center, which is for me coming to God, is my sense of private and personal guilt for injuries that I have perpetrated, sometimes deliberately, sometimes deliberately, sometimes without awareness of others for reasons that are private, that have to do with my own hurt. So that guilt and hatred and bitterness become—generate a climate, an atmosphere, a thickness by which I am surrounded psychically so that I don't know where I am in terms of—no, that's wrong—something deep within me feels that I don't have the right to experience the Presence.

And let me digress, and if I don't get back to it remind me that I left it somewhere down the road. I'll try to get back to it. When I refer to God, I am not talking about a thing, I am not talking about an object: I am talking about a Presence. Now what on earth is a Presence? Well, the mind certainly needs—I'm having a hard time to try to break this down so that you can see what I think I see. The mind deals with ultimate ideas, with ultimate concepts analogously; you can't—in the same way that we deal with ourselves. If I were to ask you: Who are you? What would you tell me? What would you say? Oh, I'm my mother's son; or I'm my mother's daughter; I'm my child's father or mother; I'm my brother's sister or my sister's brother. But who are you? You can only define you, if I may use the wrong word, define, in terms that are analogous, some image that the mind can handle but you know that the image is not the thing itself but it is a way of thinking about the thing itself; it is a way of feeling about the thing itself, because there is an aspect of the mind, a dimension of the mind that itself is ultimate. And therefore when the mind tries to think of that which is ultimate it can only do it with a series of "for instances."[4]

When the devout rabbi thinks of the King of the Universe and he uses the word King of the Universe, or the God of Abraham, Isaac and Jacob, or in some Christian disciplines the God of Jesus, or the God of my mother, my father, or my minister, always the mind has to reduce concepts, insights to manageable units. And if you keep using analogies in correspondence, somewhere along the way you will hit an analogy and

---

4. See Thurman's discussion of symbols in HT, "Mysticism and Social Change," in PHWT 2: 199–200.

you'll see light come in the person's face because, "Ah, I understand now what you are meaning by what you are saying." So that when I use the term God, I am doing the best I can with that which can't be encapsulated. So the most convenient way for me is to think in terms of Presence, or I may use, because of my own background, Spirit.

When I was growing up in Florida ghosts were a part of your vocabulary. If you didn't believe in them you were afraid to say you didn't because one might come to visit you, you know. It was one of those things. And there were two kinds of ghosts and I was acquainted with both: ghosts that really materialized. There were ghosts that took on physical form, that were like somebody who was dead, you know, some image, and then there were ghosts that did not ever materialize but they were presences in the atmosphere. Now how could you tell? You were going along the road and suddenly a wave of hot air swept—you knew that was the presence of a ghost. I mean hot air in Florida, which meant that it had a particular hotness, I mean different from the general climate of heat, and you knew now that you were in the presence of a ["haint"] . . . and you hoped that it would go on, I mean pass by.[5]

But . . . Presence: it is something that emanates from. For if I could define, if I could concretize in words what I mean by God then it means that I can reduce that which is ultimate in my mind to something else. Then that thing to which I reduce it would be ultimate. So how do we get along then? We talk of that which cannot be spoken in symbols that will indicate what we are about in our thinking and in our minds but cannot verbalize. So that—and that is why in my thought about God I cannot reduce it to a thought. So the language that I use, God is Creator—and at once you think of somebody creating. But I feel the borning process, I feel the borning process. And I use the word borning rather than creating process because that just brings to mind . . . the borning process. So, when I say in my thought God is Creator, when I spell it out so that I can get handles for my mind, Creator of Life. Well, life is not an abstract term in my mind, it is concrete. It is a tree or dog or cat or you or me: it is something that has certain characteristics that I recognize as living as

---

5. For Thurman's childhood experience of ghosts, see Peter Eisenstadt, *Against the Hounds of Hell: A Life of Howard Thurman* (Charlottesville: University of Virginia, 2021), 37.

over against dead. But that in itself is too concrete because life, to be life, has to particularize itself in a tree or in a cat or in something. I can't just think life. So my mind goes a step back: I think of God as the Creator of the Living Substance, the Life Stuff out of which any particular expression that has form and place and properties that mind can handle, that— it is comparatively simple in my thinking for me to say that God creates a particular because I am accustomed to seeing particular things come out of a certain kind of creative process. So that my mind can't rest there so that I must push it back by saying that God is the Creator of the Living Stuff, the substance out of which particular expressions of life arise. The Life Stuff that spawns units that can be defined in time and place and space. But that places a limitation, so that I push it, my mind pushes it further, and it says that God is the Creator of Existence.

Now I take a cosmic leap, and that's all time-space manifestations of any kind of reality. What do I mean when I say that a thing exists? What am I talking about? It has properties. It has a quality that separates itself from my own being so that it can be a predicate. It can be a predicate of which life is the subject so that I can think objectively about it as if I were not it and it were not I. But yet that doesn't satisfy this hunt of my mind that's been hounding me ever since I can remember consciousness. That leaves something outside that can't be included when I just use the word existence. So I come upon phrases like this, and here I am resting until I can't rest here any longer: that God bottoms existence—bottoms it—bottoms it! And that seems to satisfy me for a while; how long I don't know. It means then that there is no thing, no form, no expression, no thisness or thatness that is not bottomed. So when I come down through the cat or through the poison ivy or through the persons in the world that I love or those that I hate: whenever I start trying to find out where the thing became available above the surface so that my consciousness could relate to it in terms that would make me establish the kind of psychological distance between me and it so I could think about it, whenever I come to anything of that sort, I know that it has to be rooted, it has to be bottomed, it has to have ground in the metaphysical or philosophic sense. So I find it helpful for my structure to think of God as bottoming existence so that there is no available expression having to do with anything that is outside of that.

Now the curiously interesting thing to me (and I'll really get back to sin in a minute unless this is—what I am doing is regarded as sin. I don't know. You might). You know last night when I was having great difficulty trying to go to sleep because there were a lot of little things about the baseball game that made life uncomfortable for me. Well I won't say any more about it. So I was trying to get it out of my system. And I found it very convenient; I began thinking about you. You know I picked out various faces and it really was interesting! You would be surprised what you are saying to me. Well!

How to think in terms that are ultimate when the process of thought itself is a limiting thing. Do you see what I am trying to say? So you do the best you can because the mind insists that reality cannot be separated from some kind of limitation, some boundary. Because there is no boundary you can't—what's the word I want?—you can't draw a bead on it. And this is universal. So that in Greek philosophy, for instance, in Aristotle. And the only way that I can be aware of the universal is through the particular. And as fundamental, Platonism insists that the only reality is the universal and any orthodox Aristotelian that the only reality is the particular; and it moves all the way through.[6]

In Christianity what is God like? He clothed himself in particular: gave to the universal a handle and the name of the handle is Jesus Christ. In Gnosticism, for instance, that gave Christianity so much trouble, almost choked it to death, you had a figure—they created a figure which was borrowed from this Greek heritage called the demiurge.[7] Now what

---

6. Plato (428–348 BCE) and his pupil Aristotle (384–322 BCE) were the two greatest figures in ancient Greek philosophy. They disagreed over the metaphysical reality of universals, the so-called Platonic Forms.

7. For Plato in his later dialogues, the *demiurge* was the benevolent fashioner of the universe. For the Gnostics, a diverse group of religious sects in early Christianity and Judaism in the first centuries after 70 CE, the demiurge was often the evil, demonic creator of the physical universe, as opposed to a higher unknowable God, creator of the ultimate reality. Thurman is correct in his brief reference to the demiurge, but his comments veil a sensitive and complex history in Christian thought. The demiurge, in Plato's accounting from *Timaeus*, written ca. 360 BCE, is a benevolent, divine craftsman who imposed order and rationality on the chaos of the material world. In Gnosticism, however, the demiurge is generally depicted as a malevolent and ignorant being who was antagonistic to the supreme creator. Early Christian heretics such as Valentinus (second century CE) and his followers taught that the demiurge created the material

was the demiurge in Gnosticism? The demiurge well, here I go—was a creature but he wasn't all creature—I have to talk about it and I can't talk about it without creaturizing it but. . . . So that when he faced the universal, when he faced the heavens, when he faced that which is timeless, the demiurge became timeless: when he faced the time-space expression, the matter like the earth, he became material. So that it depended upon which way he faced. But at one expression you got both of these things. So that this is the problem that's inherent in trying to rationalize the integrity of the religious experience which is at the heart of what the mystic is talking about.

Now it may be that you take the same principles, you take the same principles and apply them in the philosophy of the heart. What is, in essence, the aesthetic experience? It is when you are led through this expression of beauty, this exquisite shape to what? To a pulse beat that merely takes the form of Rodin's "Hand of God"[8] or somebody else's something. But if you go through the door, which is the manifestation, you come upon that great inchoate throbbing vitality. When you siphon off some of its energy so as to make it available for you in your time-space involvement you give it a name—and what is the name? The name springs from your sense of the utilitarian aspect of the thing you have your hands on. But push it all the way back and you come into the vast nameless ebb and flow where there is no time and no space, only being. And here again I am limiting it. But I have to find some way by which with my little mind I can find correspondence with it so as to get enough of it to provide a mirror into which you can look to find out what I am talking about.

Now, forgive the vast digression, we will come back now. (I'm sorry I found that. You know it's like some monster breathing down my neck and it was all right when I simply had my watch because half the time I can't see what it's about—but this thing is. . . . It is funny. Well, anyway.)

---

world and attributed to it a redemptive role in the process of salvation. Moreover, its relationship to clerical authority made it highly problematic for early church fathers (Elaine Pagels, *The Gnostic Gospels* [New York: Vintage Books, 1979], 37–38).

8. The French sculptor Auguste Rodin's (1840–1917) "The Hand of God" was one of Thurman's favorite examples of the aesthetic experience of spirituality. See HT, *The Search for Common Ground*, 9–10, and Oswald McCall's *The Hand of God* (New York: Harper & Brothers, 1939), one of Thurman's favorite books of meditations. See HT, "Oswald McCall," in PHWT 5: 245–49.

The thing that stands between me, that blocks my sense of homecoming, which is what the mystic is talking about. Or, in the Quaker sense, in the sense of some Quakers, centering down. That I am sensitive when I am on the search, on the hunt—driven, not merely on the hunt with my mind but driven to find some resting place that will give to my spirit a sense at last of being at home in the world. So that I can get rid of the sense of being a pilgrim on my way somewhere. This is what, after all, whatever our language is, whatever our culture, this is in essence what the quest of the mystic is. And this is the point of meditation, whether it is QMR or LMT or EST,[9] all whatever it is, when you shake it down, they are trying to help you find home for your spirit. So we need not bother about the terminology, and this is not the same thing as saying "all roads go to Rome" and "all things are equal!" Don't run off with this and generalize it, just remember what I am saying and how I am saying it. So that when the mystic then is using meditation, its fundamental purpose as I mentioned some time ago is detachment from the things that throw it off, that takes the soul off the scent and the scent is where? The scent is in the mystic, he is seeking what he has. It's like, you know in the East Indian who was in the University of Wisconsin, who wrote *My Brother's Face*[10]—you know. Don't you know? Oh, shucks—anyway, *My Brother's Face*, and he talks about the musk deer in North India. And he says that in the springtime the deer (what's the baby of a deer? Fawn? Now what is next, doe? Now doe is female, is that right? Well anyway . . .). The baby deer in the springtime is haunted

---

9. Thurman was referring to various programs within the Human Potential Movement of the 1960s and 1970s, such as QMR (Quantum Meditation and Relaxation) and EST (Erhard Seminar Training). LMT is a common abbreviation for licensed massage therapists.

10. Dhan Gopal Mukerji (1890–1936) was one of the first successful Indian writers in the United States. His *Gay Neck, the Story of a Pigeon* (New York: E. P. Dutton, 1927) won the Newberry Medal for the year's best book in children's literature. *My Brother's Face* (New York: E. P. Dutton, 1924), 140–41, discusses the ancient Indian legend of the musk deer, a group of several species of small deer, living near the Himalayas, highly prized (and now, as a result, highly endangered), that chase their own scent. Mukerji never taught at the University of Wisconsin. For musk deer, see *For the Inward Journey: The Writings of Howard Thurman* (ed. Anne Spencer Thurman; intro. Vincent Harding; New York: Harcourt Brace Jovanovich, 1984), 54.

by the odor of musk. It's in his nostrils; it just drives him mad; it puts a fever in his blood that cannot be cured until at last he can saturate himself with all of the vitality of musk. So he runs everywhere, around every bush, every tree, crossing every rivulet, sniffing—just wild. This blood drives him insane—the fever in his blood does, until he falls exhausted with his head resting on his paw trying to get his air. Then what does he discover? That the odor of musk is in his own skin. This is what I am talking about. I hunger for God, says the mystic, and it is God hungering for himself in me. So whatever seems to block this— back where I started, now—that locks up my sinuses, I must get it out of the way. Hence the discipline, hence the real anatomy of meditation initially. And one of the things of which he is aware is the wrongdoing in his own life—the sin. Not particularly the injury, so much the injury, so much the injury that he has caused someone else, that may be a part of it, but where in his private life the person has violated what in the private life is recognized as being that which is right, true for the individual. Not the accusing finger that someone points because you did this or that, you can handle that, you know, and there are various ways to negotiate. You can find out the other person isn't so holy either, you know. But you can't negotiate with yourself. You can't do it without knowing that somewhere along the way you have decided to look the other way in you and . . . [break in class session].

The new mother when she looks at the head of the babe in her arms whispers in her heart, "My child, may you seek after truth. If anything I teach you be false, may you throw it from you and go on to richer truths and deeper knowledge than I have ever known. If you become a man of thought and learning, may you never fail to tear down with your right hand what your left hand has built up through years of thought and study if you see it at last not to be founded on that which is. If you become a politician, may no success for your party or love of your nation ever lead you to tamper with reality and to play a diplomatic part. If you become an artist, may you never paint with pen or brush any picture of external life otherwise than as you see it. In all of your circumstances, my child, fling yourself down on the truth and cling to that [like] a drowning man in a stormy sea flings himself on a plank and clings to it knowing that whether he sinks or swim with it, it is the best that he has. Die poor, unknown, unloved, a failure, perhaps, but shut your eyes to nothing that seems to them the reality." Now, that's Olive Schreiner. . . .[11]

Now we are talking about, I mean we are thinking about the thing that blocks the mystic when in his meditation or in her meditation there appears straight across his passageway, his roadway, that which sends him back or holds him up. The whole point of detachment is this.

One of the roadblocks, one of the things that stands in his way is the way in which, in his private life, he sees himself; however the language may be, whatever language he may use, he sees himself as a sinner, as a guilty person whether the guilt has been named by anybody or not; whether or not any accusing finger has pointed. This is easy to handle because you can negotiate. And if you can't negotiate, you can always decide the other person is wrong—they really don't know what it's all about. "If I knew you and you knew me, if each of us could clearly see by that inner light divine, the meaning of your life and mine, I'm sure that we would differ less and clasp our hands in friendliness—If I knew you and you knew me."[12] But you don't know me, so therefore it's your fault. You see, that's easy, you negotiate this. But I'm not talking about that. I'm talking about that which stands revealed when I am stripped to whatever there is in me that is literal and irreducible. When I am looking at my own inner nakedness this thing is there, and it stands between me and my own center where he dwells. And the mind does all kinds of things with this. So I am driven finally now to come to grips with that which I and I alone know to be clouding my vision, blocking my path. And I try to find a way to remove it. And whatever my religious traditions or perhaps even whatever my cultural tradition is I bring to bear on this process everything that I can get that has to do with spot removing, you know. You find this. . . . And I can remove everything but the stain, the stain.

So how do I go at it? How does the mystic go at it? Nothing tremendous or miraculous about it. The first thing that he has to do is to name it—name it, name it. The second thing that he has to do is to take respon-

---

11. "The New Mother" in HT, "From Man to Man," in *A Track to the Water's Edge: The Olive Schreiner Reader* (ed. Howard Thurman; New York: Harper & Row, 1973), 153. For Schreiner and Thurman, see Eisenstadt, *Against the Hounds of Hell*, 90–96.

12. "If I Knew You and You Knew Me," by Nixon Waterman (1859–1944).

sibility for its presence and for its power to stay put as a roadblock. And in his or her desperation, the ultimate gesture—and I use gesture not in any superficial sense, gesture as a fundamental expression of the self—is to make of this thing, this now terrible thing, terrible because of its power over me, to offer that to God, not because he can, will, may remove it but it is the only way that I can offer myself. And I trust him to do the separating. But then I have to wrestle with the traditional sense of guilt because my whole—I think the whole experience of the race is to offer the best, the best of me to God. And then I remember something: I remember that the—that if it be true (bear in mind what we were talking about whatever it was minutes ago)—if it be true that all of life is the lung through which God breathes, all of it, then whatever it is that's a part of my mixture. His concern is, and don't misunderstand me when I use these patronizing terms. Then I am thinking analogously, please remember that. His concern is to take that which is of Him out of the prison of Him which is in me. And the prison house is the thing that I am calling my sin, my—the thing I can't forgive myself for. We are dealing here with the same principle, I think, which is present in the role of suffering in the heightening or the deepening or the sense of the Presence of God in the life.

One of the great creative and redemptive roles of suffering is that God does not have to go all over the world trying to find me. All he needs to do is to get him a comfortable seat in the place where I am just screaming with pain and agony and wait. Everything in me will finally be there trying to get me off that hot seat. So if he wants to find me, this is where every bit of me I can get my hands on is summoned. So suffering is one of God's great economies. Of course, I wish he would change it a little, you know, but this is what it is.

Now to go on. So then in my meditation, in the mystic's meditation, he finds himself moving from whatever may be the process of meditation, the stripping, all of this, into prayer, into prayer. I've puzzled over this so many times in my own journey—how sometimes in what I call meditation I'm getting the things removed that would give me more and more of a sense of detachment and without ever being aware of when it happened, I find myself praying—I mean doing what I call praying. What I am trying to say to you, and I don't want to confuse you—I mean any more than I have been—what I am trying to say is that the purpose of meditation for the mystic is vehicular for detachment. The logic of detachment in the mystic's frame of reference is attachment—attachment.

Now sometimes when I am dealing with the things that block my passage, what I would call sins of my life, I wouldn't call them error—but the sins of my life, and there is a difference, I cry for help. I ask God not to remove it. No, No! Because the trigger of removal is in me. So I ask God to help me desire to remove it, because most of the things that are not right in my own life know that I want them to be there. It is hard for me to admit this: if I would ever relax my stranglehold on them the energy of God would sweep them out of my life on the current. But I don't want to get rid of them. And it has taken a life long, my life long to be able to admit that, admit that. Not to boast about it or not to do anything, but just to admit it.

One day I was going on the train from [downtown Los Angeles] and when the train stopped at Glendale a lady got on and all the seats were pretty well [filled], there were two or three other individual passengers riding but she chose to sit by me. And I feel that every minute of your life should be accounted for or a decision made not to account for it and that's another way of accounting for it, you see. So I had a book that I had to read between Los Angeles and San Francisco—you always . . . anyway that's the way I am. So she sat down, got herself comfortable, and I was reading my read and she grunted something; she spoke something and I said, I recognized what she had to say and never looking. It was sort of rude. I didn't ever look up, you know, I just sort of glanced a little because I didn't want her to feel that I was giving her attention because I had no intention of spending my day talking to her. But she just kept [at it]. I'd put my eyes on [the book] then she'd nibble again. So I finally decided that I would give her a half hour. So looked at my watch, looked outside, closed my book, sighed deeply, stretched like this and engaged her in conversation. And she was off to the races, said all kinds of things. And I moved in and out of her flow, you know. Finally, apropos of nothing, she turned to me and said, "Do you believe in prayer?"

And in my slow-motion way I said, "Yes."

She said, "So do I!"

Then she launched into the most fantastic thing. She said, "Before I left my house in Glendale, I had my regular morning's prayer time with

God. And I decided there was something I had been trying to do for a long time that I would take all my troubles, that had just given me so much trouble, and put them in one container, in one bag, tie them up neatly, and I handed them to God relieved at last." And, she said, "You know what happened?"

I said, "No."

She said, "Before he could get them open, I snatched them back again because I felt so uncomfortable without them."

Now this is ridiculous, but this is at the core of the discipline of detachment in order that one may experience attachment. So that when you, so you read with St. John of the Cross, [we ask] what is a dark night of the soul?[13] What is this long dark tunnel which somewhere in all the literature of whatever the mystic is, he carries in his spirit the scar tissue from the wounds that he received in the darkness, and these are his witnesses as in *Pilgrim's Progress*. Do you know that climactic thing when Pilgrim nears the great summit, that the pitcher is broken at the fountain and he says, he hears the welcoming party on the other side, and he says, "My sword—not—My wounds I take with me to show to him that I have fought his battles; my sword I leave to anybody who can handle it."[14]

Now this is a graphic way of saying that the dynamic relevancy of meditation for the mystic is vehicular. It is not an end in itself. It is so important to remember this. It is a means, but a means or course that perhaps cannot be separated from the end. I am not smart enough to know that, but I do know that it is descriptive of the way, the passage through which he goes. And the vital instrument that facilitates the rite of passage is meditation and prayer. They are not ends in themselves. And, of course, this is the temptation. There is something so exquisitely aerating to the soul about meditation when it is deeply entered into, you know. You, if you could just build a tabernacle and just stay there, and that's the trap. I am not the goal in meditation. It is not merely for the clarification of my own mind and the fumigating of my own ego. It is to swing wide the

---

13. Spanish mystic St. John of the Cross (1542–1591).

14. "My sword I give to him that shall succeed me in my pilgrimage, and my courage and him to that can get it. My marks and scars I carry with me, to be a witness for me, that I have fought His battles, who shall be my Rewarder" (John Bunyan, *Pilgrim's Progress* [1681], Part II).

door that opens into his Presence. And I come back to the contradiction and the paradox that is the key to the door I have already. (What is it that the medieval Hindu, what's his name? You know. Or do you? The medieval Hindu poet. A great Hindu mystic—Kabir!) Anyway he has a great thing that says, "I laugh when you say that a fish in the water is thirsty. Do you seek the real, the true? Go where you will from Benares up north to Mathura in the south. If you have not found your own soul, the world is unreal to you."[15] It's another way of saying it from another universe of discourse. The essence of the paradox, that when I come to him I come to myself. And perhaps... and perhaps another way of saying this is that God, the Creator of life, the living substance, the bottom of existence has only one great unfinished task in his creation and that is to come to himself in all aspects of his creation: come to himself in me, in my dog, in poison ivy, in tubercular bacilli, in the wild frantic passion of cancer cells. In all of his creation he is working so he can claim himself in himself. And sometimes I think that all existence is a process by which God is engaged in trying to become self-conscious, self-conscious.

Now the mystic then uses meditation as a means to an end, not as an end in itself. And the problem which the experience of detachment creates, and understand me now, the vehicular dimension of meditation for the mystic is to achieve detachment. And to use Eckhart's great phrase that if I can empty myself of creatureliness, that is if I can experience complete detachment, God automatically will fill up the vacuum. And sometimes I don't think Eckhart is right.[16]

---

15. *Songs of Kabir* (trans. Rabindranath Tagore; New York: Macmillan, 1915), poem 43. Kabir (1440–1518) was an Indian religious poet, born in Benares, born Muslim, later a Hindu; he taught the essential unity of the two religions. Thurman quoted this poem as early as 1925; see PHWT 1: 51

16. Thurman believed that God is never at the mercy of human initiative. Thurman registers this concern here and in other places regarding Eckhart's teaching on detachment and the necessity of God filling the vacuum. For references to some of Eckhart's statements that speak to Thurman's concern, see *Meister Eckhart* (ed. Colledge and McGinn), 286: "and yet I praise detachment above all love. First, because the best thing about love is that it compels me to love God, yet detachment compels God to love me.... And I prove that detachment compels God to come to me in this way; it is because everything longs to achieve its own natural place. Now God's own natural place is unity and purity, and that comes from detachment. Therefore, God must of necessity give himself to a heart that has detachment..."; or "I say the same

The interesting thing to me is that everything that we are learning today about the nature of the external world, all the latest things that we are discovering about the nature of matter and all of this, we are coming more and more up single entities, in some language the building blocks of[17] . . . And of course this is what the mystic understands already. The danger is, to use—to take what we are discovering in the natural world as arguments for the existence of a creator or something of that sort. That's irrelevant in terms of the quest of the mystic. What the mystic is concerned about is that his sense of the presence of God that is resident and resonant at his center will find a way by which it can go home to the source of all. Or that it can become—or that the source of all can become aware of itself in me.

Now how does he know when it happens? Is there such a thing as a pragmatic test for reality? I don't know. But anything that presented itself to my mind as a test I would disbelieve because I do not think that it is possible to reduce God, reality, whatever the way, whatever the phrase you use, to reduce it to a formula. If at some time, somewhere through the eons I could write QED,[18] I would be home free. But the moment I wrote it I would feel something nudge me on the elbow saying, "You didn't include me."

Now let me tie this up. The mystic uses meditation as a means. The degree to which the experience of meditation is vital, the temptation is to use it as an end. So you have to bear that in mind in reading all this . . . whether you read in Plotinus or Eckhart or Boehme or any of these peo-

---

about the man who has annihilated himself in himself and in God and in all created things . . . God must pour out the whole of himself with all his might so totally into every man who has utterly abandoned himself that God withholds nothing of his being or his nature or his entire divinity . . ."; Sermon 48, "A Master Speaks," cited in *Meister Eckhart*, 197.

17. The passage is incomplete and perhaps garbled. Thurman seems to arguing against overly facile uses of the argument from design to argue for the existence of God, a proof that mystics would find superfluous. Thurman was certainly sympathetic to finding traces of the divine in nature, but at times he was more skeptical. "It is always dangerous to read into the behavior of nature some great design or plan to human life" (HT, *Deep Is the Hunger: Meditations for the Apostles of Sensitiveness* [1951; repr., Richmond, IN: Friends United Press, 1973], 27).

18. Acronym for the Latin phrase *quod erat demonstrandum*, literally meaning "what was to be shown."

ple, remember this is a part of the problem with which they are wrestling. Even in the biblical, the Christian tradition this was the problem with Jesus all the time. And think of what must have been the horrendous terror (can those two words go together? I guess they can. Horrendous terror—it's a . . . well anyway, I'll use it and you can decide I don't know what I am talking about. So that's all right. I know what I am talking about) that must have been just flowing through him like salt through an open wound, when on the cross in the oldest of the Gospels the last words that he utters as he is dying, "My God, My God, Why hast thou forsaken me?" All this other business has been added later, "Father, into thy hands I give my spirit," or what the christologists have done with it, and it is all right, it serves a purpose. That I have followed the relentless logic of the path that opened up before my view and at every critical point where all of me shouted for your imprimatur, your approval, you were there—Peter's mother's dying, some other girl dead, transfiguration when I had this psychic moment when it seemed to me that all the ends tied together in Abraham, Isaac, and somebody. Well, anyway there were these people. You were there. In the garden where I was just raising every kind of thing I could because I didn't want to die; you were there and you nudged me quietly on the elbow and whispered in my ear, "You must do my will." I heard you. Now here I am up here dying and the pain is so overwhelming that my consciousness dips and I black out and I climb these hills of pain again and I become conscious hoping now this next time I come up you'll be there: where on earth are you? And he died screaming this. And in the heart of it, in the heart of it, perhaps he was making the supreme discovery of his life. That I am surest of him when he seems farthest removed from me. This may be the heart of the paradox not only of religious experience but the heart of the paradox of the mystic's moment before he enters into what all of the mystics—whatever may be their language—recognize as union—union, union. And this may be the only way by which it can come. I don't know, I don't know. But I do know that I seem to be surest of God when he seems farthest removed from me. What the paradox is I don't know. I've spent a life-long time trying to fathom it: I don't know. But it is when I seem so sure of this Presence that suddenly he isn't there anymore—I am left hanging. Not always but too many times for comfort or reassurance. So many times when there seems to be a desert and a sea between me and an awareness of his Presence in my spirit then I blink and here he is. And the thing that is so overwhelmingly shocking and embarrassing to me is that often when such is my experience, I feel that he has caught me—he has come, I become aware of him when nothing is in order, when nothing is in order. If I could have just had a premonition, but right in the middle sometimes of something that I am doing that is completely spiritually devitalizing and utterly humiliating, I hear, to use a figure, the movement of his wings.

You know you think of the most ridiculous things. You'll just have to put up with me; I didn't ask you to register for this course, so you just do the best you can. I have no responsibility for you. But in the days of the First World War, when they went through the South and collected as many male Black seniors in high school as possible to come to the nation's capital to give them three months of intensive military infantry drill regulation training so they could go back to their high schools and teach the fellows the infantry drill regulation so when they were drafted they would have a technique and a skill that would be a kind of shield against the sort of sadistic stuff to which they were exposed in the army way back then, well for a lot of reasons, I don't want to go into that but they are good reasons. So somebody conceived of the idea if you could bring these fellows in then when they were drafted they would know the infantry drill regulations, and you could start out as being second sergeants, and this would stand between the sadism of the regular officers and the regular non-commissioned officers and these rank people from Florida, Alabama, Mississippi. So I was from my high school, and we were learning these infantry regulations. We were sitting on the hillside at the university, you know we were on a university campus, down in a sort of pocket, and the field officer would be explaining something: how do you do correctly an about face and all this sort of thing, and then suddenly the second lieutenant in charge of us would holler, "Attention!" and we would jump up and stand at attention; because at that moment he smelled the particular kind of perfume that the second lieutenant wore.[19] So, he was smelling before he emerged, so you knew when he

---

19. For Thurman's time in the Student Army Training Corps in the summer of 1918, spent at an encampment at Howard University, see Eisenstadt, *Against the Hounds of Hell*, 56–57.

turned the corner we'd be all ready. Well, it's a terrible analogy, but there is a dimension that's illustrative of what I am talking about in this. There is a holy immanence that goes . . . [Thurman, reminded that the class was supposed to stop at eleven o'clock, abruptly ends the class without finishing his sentence.]

Mysticism and Social Change: Rufus Jones

25 July 1978
Pacific School of Religion

In 1956, Howard Thurman wrote to Rufus Jones's biographer, Elizabeth Vining, about his time studying with Rufus Jones at Haverford College in 1929:[1]

I can only say that the period that I spent guided by his mind and spirit in my reading and study marked the watershed of my whole life. It was he who first opened up to me the world of mystical religion as it has been witnessed in the literature of the faith.

It was far more exciting than I have words to express to discover what I had sensed and experienced in my own spiritual journey was a part of the movement of God in the life of man through the ages. It was as if I was surrounded by a cloud of witnesses which gave to me a sense of belonging that the madness and terror to which I was exposed in America could not undermine.

Thurman's six months studying with Jones was a watershed in his intellectual and spiritual development.[2] *Before studying with Jones, Thurman's understanding of mysticism was largely intuitive. Thereafter, he was conscious of being part of a specific mystic tradition, one taught to him by Jones; and many of the leading mystics in Jones's personal canon, such as Meister*

---

1. HT to Elizabeth Vining, 18 April 1956, Folder 8, Box 35, HTC.
2. For accounts of Thurman's study with Jones, see PHWT 1: lxviii–lxix; Luther E. Smith Jr., *Howard Thurman: The Mystic as Prophet* (1981; repr., Richmond, IN: Friends United Press, 2006), 33–38; Eisenstadt, *Against the Hounds of Hell*, 111–15.

Eckhart, became favorites of Thurman. Jones also introduced Thurman to Quaker worship practices and the long Quaker history of combining spiritual inspiration with social activism, what Jones called *affirmation mysticism*, contrasting it to *negation mysticism*, a mysticism that shuns contact with the outside world.[3]

Thurman often wrote about his study with Jones.[4] The following lecture, given in July 1978 as part of a course "Mysticism and Social Change" at the Pacific School of Religion, in Berkeley, California, is his most extended, and frankest, account of his study with Jones.[5] The lecture focuses on their interactions, Jones's personality, his ambivalences and simultaneous embrace of both a parochially Christian and a universal understanding of the Quaker doctrine of the inner light. Thurman lectured on what he saw as the contradiction between Jones's intense commitment to worldwide social activism and his seeming indifference to the situation of Black Americans in the United States. Nonetheless, he felt that Jones transcended his limitations. "Here was a man," said Thurman, "to whom the angels had spoken and into whose ears God has whispered, and I could trust his words." While "in his presence you felt that you were in the presence of a great spirit," but also "*felt that you were a great spirit*" too.

Today I begin another approach. I want to talk with you about Rufus Jones.[6] I went entirely through seminary without ever hearing the

---

3. For Thurman on Jones and affirmation mysticism, see "Mysticism and Social Change" (February 1939) in PHWT 2: 214.

4. See WHAH 74–77; "Men Who Have Walked with God: Rufus Jones," 24 September 1950, Folder 64, Box 11, HTC. See also Thurman's Rufus Jones Memorial Lecture, published as *Mysticism and the Experience of Love* (Wallingford, PA: Pendle Hill, 1961). At Howard University, Thurman taught special seminars on Rufus Jones (see PHWT 2: xxx).

5. HT, "Mysticism and Social Change #12," (25 July 1978), Folder 38, Box 8, HTC.

6. Rufus Jones (1863–1948) was born in Maine into a Quaker family. He attended Haverford College, a Quaker college outside Philadelphia, and graduated in 1885, staying on for an additional year for an MA. He completed his education by obtaining a second MA at Harvard University in 1901, studying with William James and Josiah Royce. He began teaching at Haverford in 1893 and remained there for his entire career. In 1917 he was a co-founder of the American Friends Service Committee

name Rufus Jones and therefore without coming in contact with any of his works. I first encountered him in a little book, as I mentioned to you once before, called *Finding the Trail of Life*.[7] I knew, at a level in my mind and perhaps in my spirit also, that if this man were living he is the man with whom I want to spend some time. I had abandoned all of the delusions of study without being, of course, overwhelmed by the insights, but I had abandoned the delusions and I did not want to study anything else for its own sake.[8] I wanted to find out what kind of footprints did God make in a man's mind. And if I could trace those, then perhaps I could find out on what he was the scent of, if I may put it that way. And it may be I would recognize it in a way that was native to my own life and need. I had no idea where to start, how to get in touch with him; but as I mentioned, I think to you before, in the fall of that year [1928] I went to the University of Pennsylvania to do worship in their Freshman Camps. They had a camp out at Green Lane[9] or Green Lake, someplace like that, where all freshman of the university came for a week of orientation. And a part of the orientation was to give these freshmen an hour every morning dealing with some aspect of the inner life or religion or that whole business. So, I was asked to come over from Ohio to do this. And after about the third day one of the men there invited me to visit the following winter, to visit his meeting. It was the first live Quaker that I'd ever encountered. I had been acquainted, of course, with Whittier,[10] and you know, I knew some of it up here, but I hadn't touched a live Quaker. And I said, "Do you know a man whose name is Rufus Jones?"

(AFSC) and served as its chairman or honorary chairman for the remainder of his life. Over the next three decades Jones took numerous overseas trips to further its work, and he played a significant role in helping to provide food and other forms of assistance to Europe in the aftermath of World War I. See Elizabeth Gray Vining, *Friend of Life: The Biography of Rufus M. Jones* (Philadelphia: Lippincott, 1958).

7. Rufus M. Jones, *Finding the Trail of Life* (New York: MacMillan, 1926). One reason why Thurman was so impressed by Jones's book is that it is about the religious awakening of a young boy through contacts with nature, with many parallels to Thurman's own early development.

8. Thurman by 1928 had made the difficult decision not to pursue a doctorate. See Eisenstadt, *Against the Hounds of Hell*, 107–8.

9. Green Lane and Green Lane Park are about forty miles north of Philadelphia.

10. The Quaker poet John Greenleaf Whittier (1807–1892).

And when he recovered from the stupidity of the question, because he assumed that everybody in heaven and above and beyond knew Rufus. And he said, "Well, we've been friends forty years, and we are neighbors, etc."

And then I said, "You know, I wonder whether or not I could come and hang around him for a while because I'd like to do this. I want to.... I don't want to study anything other than that which moves with the grain in my own wood."

And he said, "I don't know. I'm sure Rufus has never done anything like this, but when I go back home, I will call him up or I will go to see him and tell him." He asked me for my address, my name, all the rest of it, and in about two days, three days, I get this one-page letter from Rufus in that measured, Hamilton-hand handwriting,[11] you know that ... you know very ... And "Dear Friend," That's how it began and he said, "I hear from friend so and so and so that thee has some idea, and write and tell me what it is."

So, I wrote him this letter and I told him. It was a great letter.[12] I told him how old I was, what my educational training was, what I was doing now, why I wanted to spend some time in the presence of a mind and a spirit like his. I also told him, "I don't know what the attitude of your school is about me because I'm a Black boy ... and my color is black," I said, "so that if I go everybody will know that I'm there. So, I don't want you to have any whatever-it-is that you could have about it."[13]

Well by return mail I got this letter in which he said he had never done this before, but he was very much interested in it. He was sorry I didn't write him two months before because if I'd written him two months before I could have gotten a grant of some sort because Haverford College had given up its graduate school but the endowment of the

---

11. Probably a reference to the American politician Alexander Hamilton (1757–1804), who had a much admired and emulated elegant, clear, and flowing cursive handwriting.

12. Unfortunately little of the early correspondence between Jones and Thurman is extant, and none of the papers he wrote for Jones survive; but see Thurman to Rufus M. Jones, 4 June 1929, in PHWT 1: 152–53.

13. From the late nineteenth century until 1947, Haverford College admitted only one Black student, recruited for the cricket team. Thurman was admitted as a special student.

graduate school was now being used to give scholarships to men who wanted to do the master's degree in one, two, or three fields. "But," he said, "you can have a room in Graduate House. And I don't know what else to say," the letter said.

So, I answered at once telling him I would come in January and to reserve this room in Graduate House for me, and that was it. So, I went in January. It was the first year that Doug Steere,[14] that name may be familiar to some of you, began his teaching at Haverford, and he lived up on the top floor, and I had a room on the first floor. And was my first introduction to four o'clock tea. You know, this drove me mad because usually Doug, who'd spent two years at Oxford, would put out this stuff and you would sit with tea and talk—well, that was off the point—at any rate I did what I could with it. And when I met Rufus it was a very great moment. He was six feet, easily six feet, walked in a subdued gallop, you know. When he lectured, he rocked, so that every three months they would take that chair out and put another chair in with brads[15] under it.

He taught freshman and sophomore psychology and philosophy. And when we met, I got his permission to attend all of his classes so that every time he opened his mouth, for six months, I was in the group. There was a Silent Meeting at Haverford at the meetinghouse on Wednesdays, and every Wednesday the spirit moved Rufus to talk. So that you knew if he were present, he was going to talk. So that was one more thing. He had a special seminar for professors of philosophy at Bryn Mawr and Temple and Penn and Swarthmore on Meister Eckhart,[16] and I attended that every Tuesday night. And once a week we would sit to talk. At first, we simply talked. I was trying to find out where I was in my own thinking and what on earth is mysticism. And little by little I began to discover

---

14. Douglas Van Steere (1901–1995) taught at Haverford College from 1928 to 1964. His many works on Quaker religion and spirituality include *On Listening to Another* (New York: Harper, 1955) and *Dimensions of Prayer* (New York: Harper & Row, 1963). Thurman reviewed Steere's *On Beginning from Within* in 1944, in PHWT 3: 94–96. See also Douglas V. Steere, "Don't Forget Those Leather Gloves," in *Essays in Honor of Howard Thurman on the Occasion of His Seventy-Fifth Birthday, November 18, 1975* (ed. Samuel Lucius Gandy; Washington, DC: Hoffman, 1976).

15. Thin, flattish nails.

16. See HT, "Mysticism and Social Change: Meister Eckhart," printed in the current volume.

that what he was talking about I had known all my life, but it had not been defined and made articulate in any way. But to give it a category was something a little awkward.

So anyway, without taking too much time on that, he also guided my reading. He would suggest lots of material. For instance, one whole period was spent in reading the Spanish Mystics.[17] And then at my suggestion I asked if he would let me write a paper giving my reactions to these people, and he agreed to do that. And then a whole series on the different Catholic Orders, and to do two or three things—studies for him of Madame Guyon, because I was fascinated by the fact that there seems to be just a thin line between a sense of God, a sense of Presence in your spirit, in your mind and being a little off.[18] That I didn't know anything then, don't know much now; but I didn't know anything then so that I was curious, I began to draw back because I remember saying to Rufus one afternoon in our talk together, "I recognize the spiritual thing that's here, but," I said, "why are all these people sort of this way."

And he didn't comment, but he gave me a book to read, Leuba, *Psychology of Mysticism*. Is that it? Somebody knows that book. It's a standard on.... Well anyway he gave it to me to read. And in it there was a detailed discussion by a psychologist at Bryn Mawr, on the balance, and how the emotional intensity again and again of mystical experience tended to put the mind in a tilted place.[19] That's one part of it. I was fascinated by St. Francis. I, so I asked him would he let me do a long definitive paper of St. Francis, and he did. Oh my, it must have been seventy-five, eighty pages, and one of the great experiences of my life was going through all the literature that I could read and all of the materials having to do with the life of this strange and fascinating and sometimes, to me, terribly embarrass-

---

17. Primarily St. Teresa of Avila (1515–1582) and St. John of the Cross (1542–1591).

18. Madame Guyon (1648–1717), the inspiration for the French Catholic tradition of Quietism, emphasized the importance of prayer and contact with God. Her views were condemned by the French Catholic hierarchy, and she was imprisoned from 1695 to 1703, spending several years in the Bastille.

19. James H. Leuba, *The Psychology of Mysticism* (London: Kegan Paul, Trench, Treubner, 1925). In the chapter "The Great Mystics, Hysteria, and Neurasthenia" Leuba argues that many of the great mystics—his chapter is largely limited to female mystics, including Madame Guyon—"suffered from hysterical attacks" (191).

ing human being, because he had gone so far on a road that I was trying to find on the map.[20]

Occasionally Rufus would give a special lecture to his freshmen. And one day he gave a lecture, a two-hour lecture, on Hegelian logic. He wanted to give them a taste of what they were going to be getting as sophomores. And I went, and it was a fantastic thing because he had these freshmen in the aisles, you know. It was a riotous thing. Every time he attempted to develop any theme, he would put a window there that was just so graphic that you had to laugh, you know. So, at the end, when the class was over, I went by the library to pick up a book before supper, and I saw the young fellow who sat by me poring over the dictionary. And I said, "I saw you at Rufus's lecture. What are you doing?"[21] He said, "I'm trying. . . . As soon as the lecture was over, I darted up here to get the two volumes of Hegelian logic out of the library because if it's that funny I want to read it." And he said, "now I'm looking up the meaning of the word "the," because the way Hegel uses it, it must be different from any [other.]"

So in my next meeting with Rufus, I said, "How does it happen that you are able to take these tremendously creative and apparently timeless concepts and reduce them to manageable units so that the simple mind can grasp it and see what you are talking about?" And he told me a very interesting thing. He said, "I don't think that you understand an idea until you are able to put it in language in reach of the simplest mind. That's the first thing and second, he said, "I learned this in a very hard school." And he told me about the year when he was graduated from Haverford and his class was a very radical class, one of the first radical classes coming out of Haverford. And one of the tests of their radical business was that all the fellows in the class who were Quakers, and that was about 90 percent of them, wore a moustache. And when you see Whittier's picture, for instance, he has the flowing beard but no moustache, because only evil can come from underneath a lip that has a moustache on it, you know. So, he said, "All of our fellows wore moustaches. Our class invited

---

20. For St. Francis, see HT, "Men Who Have Walked with God: St. Francis," printed in the current volume.

21. The philosophy and logical system of Georg Wilhelm Friedrich Hegel (1770–1831) were notoriously abstruse.

Mathew Arnold to lecture in the United States and he was way out," as Rufus put it.[22]

[He continued,] "And that year, at the end of my senior year, I was invited to Cleveland to meet, to talk on the First Day at the Friend's Meeting in Cleveland, and I made a good sermon, you know. And when I finished there were three comments made: One, by a lady who sat on the facing bench with me and the head of the meeting. And she said, "We enjoyed thee, even though what thee had to say came from underneath a moustache." And then another person spoke saying that he did not have very much unction because when he stood his coat was caught in his belt, and when he sat down his coat was still caught in his belt. And the third was more important: "We enjoyed thee, friend Rufus, but one thing thee has forgotten—our blessed Lord said feed my sheep, not my giraffes."

Now, he said, "From that point on I felt that the idea was not mine until the simplest, least sophisticated mind in my audience could grasp what I was talking about." He was not a man who had, whose mind and spirit had been visited by the mystic's vision. That's the first thing I want to say about him. He did not have what may be normally recognized as ecstatic moments when he was taken out of himself and became one with some transcendent configuration or feeling tone or image or concept. His mysticism was pedestrian. And that is why in my book his mysticism had at its center an ethical core and concern. And I think of him in terms of ethical mysticism. I am not sure, I was not sure then, I've not been sure since whether or not he is what may be regarded as a Christ mystic, as was Augustine, and you could name many others, because with reference to the inner light—now this is crucial—the fundamental position of the Friends with reference to the inner light has a kind of dichotomy that runs—given the fact of the inner light, then the road branches this way and this way. One road says that the inner light is a part of the givenness of the spirit of God in all mankind, that it is not conditioned by or upon any belief, the exercise of any body of faiths, but it is the light that lighteth every man that cometh into the world, quoting the Fourth Gospel [John 1:9]. Therefore the light is generic.

---

22. Matthew Arnold (1822–1888), the English critic and poet, visited the United States during 1883 and 1884.

Now the other road is that the inner light is available or open only to the person in whom the seed of Christ is deposited; that without this deposit even the light is darkness. And those of you who are acquainted with the history of the Society of Friends will recognize how these two emphases have in some ways divided the history of the movement.[23] Rufus seemed to me to walk well, one of the things that Olive Schreiner's mother used to say about her—it was very prophetic—that when Olive walked down the path one foot would be in the path and the other foot would be in the bushes.[24] You know she couldn't bring herself to put both feet in the path. So that I think this seems to be, I don't want to be unfair, but this seems to me to be Rufus's business because when you read his material—and at Haverford they called him the Book of the Month Club, you know, because he wrote so many books.[25] But, it seems to me in some of his writings he is profoundly a Christ mystic; that there is a moment in the life when the experience with Christ moves to the center of one's aspiration, thought, activity, commitment. Up to that time one moves in darkness.[26]

---

23. Elias Hicks (1748–1830), a Long Island Quaker, promoted the Inner Light as the ultimate source of personal spiritual authority, while Orthodox Quakers emphasized biblical authority. Starting with the Philadelphia Yearly Meeting in the late 1820s, many Quaker meetings split into rival Hicksite and Orthodox factions. Haverford College was founded by the Orthodox Philadelphia Yearly Meeting in 1833. Nearby Swarthmore College was founded by the Hicksite Yearly Meetings of Philadelphia, New York, and Baltimore in 1869. The adjacent women's college, Bryn Mawr, was founded by Orthodox Quakers in 1885.

24. For Olive Schreiner (1855–1920), the South African feminist, pacifist, novelist and social theorist, and Schreiner's influence on Thurman, see HT, ed., *A Track to the Water's Edge*.

25. Jones was the author of fifty-seven books published during his lifetime, along with hundreds of magazine and newspaper articles. In addition to his scholarly works, he was the author of numerous popular books on spirituality and helped popularize the notion of personal mysticism to a wide audience in the first half of the twentieth century. See Matthew S. Hedstrom, "Rufus Jones and Mysticism for the Masses," *Cross Currents* 52, no. 2 (Summer 2004): 31–44.

26. As an example of Jones's Christocentrism, when he met Gandhi in 1926, there was little more than strained condescension on Jones's part. Jones dismissed Gandhi as being "first, last, and always a Hindu." After giving Gandhi a failing grade for his unfamiliarity with the Quakers George Fox and John Woolman, he sniffed that Gandhi lacked both "universal interests" and a deep understanding of mysticism and saw him as clinging "to the outgrown superstition of his racial religion"; see Vining, *Friend for Life*, 219–22.

Now in some of the things that you read in Rufus that point is very clear. And in some of the other things it seems as if the light is equivalent with life. I don't want to be judgmental here, but I think it is very important that you know, if subsequently you begin reading his material, that there is this ambivalence in him. And it may be a generic ambivalence; I'm not sure because that kind of conflict creates problems that the mind can't handle. For either the light, using that phrase, is a part of the givenness of God, which is the stamp of his imprimatur on all life, or it comes as a result of some kind of participation that the individual is required to make. And if that is the case, if the latter is the case, then it means that if the individual, for whatever reasons they may be, is not able to participate in that way, that individual is cut out from the light. And this creates a very profound ethical problem, for there is something in every one of us that insists that you can't experience any good that is not available to everybody, whether the individual puts forth the effort or not. For light, however we define it, is a grace, and a grace is that which is experienced without merit: the question of merit is completely irrelevant. So that one side of the whole emphasis of Rufus is that: that to be alive is to participate in the inner light, "the light that lighteth every man," to use the Fourth Gospel quotation again, "that cometh into the world." And, of course, once you do that, then you can't stop because the light that lighteth every thing, every living thing, and you have to cut it off at some point. And what Rufus did in his thought was to limit it in a very interesting way to his sense of ethical responsibility to all human life, whether or not from his point of view, had been deposited [in] the seed of Christ. This is his mandate for developing the American Friends Service Committee, all the whole Quaker testimony in presence of pestilence and war and etc.[27] For instance, one day he said to me, "You know," he talked loud as if he wasn't quite sure that you could hear. Now he knew he could hear but he wasn't quite sure you could hear. So, he said, "Howard, do you know what I would like to do when the war is over?"

---

27. One of Jones's motivations in creating the AFSC was creating a Quaker institution that would transcend, and perhaps start to heal, internal Quaker division and sectarianism. Jones represented the AFSC in Stockholm in 1947 when it was awarded the Nobel Prize for Peace.

I said, "No, I have no idea."

"I would like to charter a big airplane and fill it full of biddies and take it to France because you can't start a civilization all over again without chickens."[28] This was Rufus.

The thing that has puzzled me, and about which only once did I talk to Rufus, was the way in which the witness of which he spoke of often, growing out of his experience with the inner light, the way that that witness concerned itself to meeting the needs of the desperate, of the destitute, of the whole, the things that came about from the ravages of war and pestilence and the guidance about the whole peace testimony. But I felt that in this emphasis it had no witness for the less dramatic, less obvious sufferings of mankind. And we talked about this a little. For instance, to illustrate what I mean, the Fellowship of Reconciliation[29] was one of the things that Rufus had a great deal of interest in, and the mainline Philadelphia Quakers supported it, but its emphasis had to do with war between nations, with war and peace, the sort of thing. It did not touch labor, so that during the period of the great Passaic, New Jersey, strikes, well those of you who've studied economic history of our country will recognize it.[30] Everybody in here is too young to know about it. But the terrible strikes at Passaic, New Jersey, textile mills and all the brutality and all that sort of thing, a great deal of pressure was put on the Fellowship of Reconciliation by mainline Philadelphia Quakers not to become involved in the economic labor struggle. And the same was true with reference to their witness about race. There was a very interesting blind spot

---

28. The conversation was held during World War II. Biddies are young chickens.

29. The Fellowship of Reconciliation was a prominent Christian pacifist organization founded in 1915.

30. The strike against textile manufacturers in Passaic, New Jersey, and nearby communities began in January 1926 and ended in March 1927, when the last of the picketed manufacturers signed a union contract. Approximately 16,000 workers were employed in the affected textile plants. The strike was instigated by the Trade Union Education League of the Workers' (Communist) Party, though during the strike, the United Textile Workers Union, affiliated with the American Federation of Labor, became the primary bargaining agent, to help facilitate a settlement. Local authorities declared martial law and employed brutal tactics to break the strike, including beatings and clubbings, tear gas, and the use of fire hoses to physically attack picketers. The strike became a cause célèbre for the American left in the 1920s.

there at this point which I found very difficult to understand. Rufus and I would talk about it now and then, but whenever we talked about it, he moved out in the great creative expanse about the meeting of human need, and I was talking about this. Please do not misunderstand me when I am saying this, but it represents one of the limping things of affirmation mysticism. It limps. For instance, to me it's rationally unbelievable that the Quaker private schools were the last private schools in the United States to admit Negroes—the last ones![31] Only one, and that was Oakwood at Poughkeepsie, New York, which was regarded by other Quaker Schools as not one of the best, [admitted Black students].[32] For years Swarthmore, when I was at Howard University I would always invite one of my friends who taught economics at Swarthmore to speak in the chapel, to keep him encouraged and inspired while he was trying to find a way by which he and his colleagues could change the policy of Swarthmore so that they would admit Negroes.[33] Bryn Mawr, even while Rufus was chairman of the board of trustees.[34] Now I'm saying all of this, not to point my finger at him, please do not misunderstand me, but what I am saying, why I am telling you this, is that it is so very difficult to keep from straining the vitality out of your commitment if you let it demand that you try to be everything to everybody. Now this is what I am trying to say to you. And the question always is then: Where do I draw the line that will permit me to make the maximum witness to the central concern of my spirit.

Now Rufus felt that he could best express this in terms of war and peace. For instance during the second year of the war, or one of the years, early, there assembled in Washington at Christmastime every year the

---

31. Whether or not Quaker-affiliated college and college preparatory schools were absolutely the last private Eastern educational institutions to admit Black students, they certainly were laggards, and Thurman was properly astonished at their collective retreat and denial of their nineteenth-century abolitionist witness.

32. The Oakwood Friends School, a college preparatory school in Poughkeepsie, New York, was founded in 1794.

33. Thurman regularly invited Patrick Malin to speak at Howard University during the 1930s, in contrast to his usual policy of not inviting speakers to Howard from institutions that did not admit Blacks (WHAH 90). Swarthmore admitted its first Black students in 1943.

34. Bryn Mawr admitted its first Black student in 1927, Enid Appo Cook, though she was obliged to live off campus. Jones was a member of the Bryn Mawr board of trustees from 1898 to 1936.

first of January a group of men who came together to pray.[35] It was called by a man whose name was Glenn Clark, who fathered Camp Further Out.[36] And Stanley Jones,[37] Rufus Jones, and some of the other people came, about eight of us, and I was living in Washington so they invited me to come. And we would spend three days out near the British embassy in a very fine house there that a lady turned over to us with tea and everything to go with it, and we would settle in, get very quiet and meditate, and then each person would express to this little group what his concern was. The main concern was we were at war. And we wanted to do this in the nation's capital because if there could be some spiritual release it might spill over to Roosevelt and these other people. While we were meeting, the second day a cable came from Europe to Rufus from the Friends Service Committee urging him to do everything he could to mobilize public opinion in the United States that would force the United States to get Churchill to break the blockade of the French coast because French children and babies were starving and they needed milk, etc.; and since England was trying to get us with this lend-lease deal, if Roosevelt really worked it he could get Churchill to lift the blockade long enough for this stuff to get in there.[38] When it came, Rufus read it to us—and Glenn

---

35. The informal prayer group met in Washington, DC, probably for the first time in 1943 on New Year's Day, and again in 1944 and 1945, by which time Thurman was in San Francisco. The group, at first confidential and private, imagined themselves as a new Pentecost, praying together to help solve the world's problems. As Thurman later indicates in the lecture, the group was too evangelical for his tastes; but when they published a volume *Together* (New York: Abingdon-Cokesbury, 1949), Thurman contributed an important essay, "God and the Race Question"; see PHWT 3: 186–90.

36. Glenn Clark (1882–1956) was for many years a professor of literature at Macalester College in St. Paul, Minnesota. In 1930 he started a summer camp and retreat that became the kernel of the Camp Farthest Out movement, and this rapidly grew to a large network of Christian summer camps. After 1942 Clark devoted himself full time to the Camp Farthest Out movement.

37. E. Stanley Jones (1884–1973) was a prominent Methodist missionary who spent many years in India. Although he was an early supporter of the interracial movement in American Christianity, Thurman was not one of his admirers; see WHAH 116, 119–20.

38. Thurman's account would place this in early 1941, when the United States had not yet entered the war, and Roosevelt and Churchill were negotiating the Lend-Lease Act, enacted in April 1941. However, as he stated shortly before, Thurman first attended the prayer group during the war, in early 1943.

Clark who was the (what do you say, chairperson?)... He was the chair-he—I mean the chair-he-she. Well, anyway, one of you wrote a paper and I'd never seen it, you'll forgive me, I'd never seen it done this way: s/he, and it opened up a whole new thing. I'd never seen that before. I don't know who did it but it—I ran upstairs to let Mrs. Thurman know she was emancipated.[39] Anyway, so immediately when this came all the other things that we'd put in the pot, about which we would pray for two hours or three hours, were just put aside. And Glenn Clark said now, let us get on the telephone to heaven and tighten the circle, and let us select the two international Joneses, Stanley Jones and Rufus Jones, to go a block and a half to the British Embassy to present this while we pray.

And I couldn't do it. I couldn't do it. So, I took my chair from the circle and sat against the wall because I could not worship a God who would jump when I pulled the strings. I couldn't trust him. They came back, and Rufus said, "I knew when I talked—when we went, we could not get a hearing with the ambassador. But we are always surrounded by the miraculous, and this may have been one of the times." And then he told something (and I'll quit now in a minute). He was with the two or three Quakers who went to Germany to see if they could get some kind of audience with Hitler, and they were put in a room to wait for more than an hour. And according to Rufus, whose sense of humor was unbelievable, "We knew that they could hear what we were saying, and that's why they put us in this room. They could listen in on our conversation. So, we went into the silence and communicated with each other [without speaking, spiritually], and there were no devices that can do that. And the curious thing, he said, "was that all the doubts that we had about the efficacy of what we were doing, each one of us who had a doubt, that doubt surfaced in the quiet and was exposed to the spirit of God and it was consumed."[40] Now—all right, we'll stop there. [class break]

---

39. This passage is an indication of how Thurman was challenged, even toward the end of his life, by the use of gender neutral language.

40. Thurman is relating the visit of Jones and two other AFSC leaders to Germany in December 1938, one month after the Kristallnacht pogrom, to see if Germany would allow the AFSC to help Jewish refugees leave Germany. (The AFSC was admired in Germany for the work it performed in feeding the hungry and destitute in the aftermath of World War I.) After arrangements were made by the US Embassy in Berlin, they had several meetings with Nazi officials, including one with Reinhard

[Then he who was my comrade hears the call
And rises from my side, and soars
Deep-chanting to the heights.]
Then I remember
And my upward gaze goes with him, and I see
Far off against the sky
The glint of golden sunlight of his wings.[41]

"I say to you," Jesus says, "cast out fear. Speak no more vain things to me about the greatness of Rome. The greatness of Rome, as you call it, is nothing but fear; fear of the past and fear of the future, fear of the poor, fear of the rich, fear of the High Priests, fear of the Jews and the Greeks, who are learned, fear of the Gauls and Goths and Huns who are barbarians, fear of the Carthage you destroyed to save you from fear of it, and now fear worse than ever, fear of Imperial Caesar, the idol you have yourself created, and fear of me, the penniless vagrant, buffeted and mocked, fear of everything except the rule of God; faith in nothing but blood and iron and gold. You, standing for Rome, are the universal coward: I, standing for the Kingdom of God have braved everything, lost everything, and won an eternal crown."[42]

My definition of Rufus is that he was an ethical mystic, one who had, until the end of his life, wrestled with fundamental ambivalences that are

---

Heydrich (1902–1942), the head of the Gestapo and one of the chief architects of the Holocaust. Jones and his colleagues received promises from the Nazi officials to allow them to do their work with refugees, and though the AFSC did play a role in helping some refugees to leave Germany, the Nazi promises proved largely worthless. When Jones returned to the United States his optimistic statements about the German government's good intentions proved controversial, though whether they reflected his true convictions or were tactical is a matter of some debate. See Rufus M. Jones, "Our Day in the German Gestapo," *The American Friend*, 10 July 1947, 265–67; Guy Aitken, "The American Friends Service Committee's Mission to the Gestapo," *Peace and Change: A Journal of Peace Research*, onlinelibrary.wiley.com/doi/pdf/10.1111/Pech12232.

41. The concluding portion of Eunice Tietjens, "The Great Man"; Eunice Tietjens (1884–1944) was a Chicago-based poet and editor.

42. Jesus, speaking to Pilate, in the preface to Shaw's "On the Rocks," in George Bernard Shaw's *Too Good to Be True, Village Wooing, and On the Rocks: Three Plays* (New York: Dodd, Mead, 1934), 228, For an earlier instance of Thurman using the quotation, from March 1939, see PHWT 2: 235n2.

inherent first, as I mentioned earlier, but to repeat it, between the light that is the givenness of God to his creation and the light that becomes available to sentient creatures, as it were, only by embracing the life, the salvation, the redemptive power and grace of Jesus Christ. He walked down these two roads all the time. His enormous captivation with Greek philosophy, with Roman thought, with the whole sweep of the contribution that during his period the natural sciences were beginning to make to man's understanding of man and the earth. All of these things were clamoring for a central place, a central motivating energy for his one passion, which was to relieve the misery of human beings created by violences that human beings wrought upon each other. He had a profound mistrust, and this is another one of his ambivalences, he had a profound mistrust of the powers of the mind and an absolute devotion to the powers of the mind. He—how can I put this—he felt that always the role of the thinker was to put at the disposal of the motivations of his life the best fruits of learning and the mastery of the external world. But this should be done best if the individuals who were seeking it would be inwardly motivated. This is so important in understanding him—inwardly motivated, not ambitiously oriented. I have to put it that way. It is for this reason, for instance, that he was one of the masterminds creating Pendle Hill at Wallingford, Pennsylvania. You are acquainted with Pendle Hill, are you? Oh my! Well, let me tarry a second. First of all Pendle Hill is the hill on which George Fox had his vision, you know, in England, you know. On Pendle Hill he saw this vision and he saw the angel with the flaming swords; and when he came down from the heights of Pendle Hill, as he puts it, "All the world had a new smell." So that Pendle Hill is one of the holy places in the mind of the history of American, English, and European mysticism, for that matter.[43] So that a group of people, led by Rufus Jones primarily and a British Quaker—mmmm, I can see him but

---

43. Pendle Hill is in East Lancashire, England. On it, in 1647, George Fox (1624–1691), the founder of the Society of Friends, or the Quakers, had a revelation, in which he "was come up in the spirit through the flaming sword into the paradise of God. All things were new, and all of the creation gave another smell to me than before, beyond what worlds could utter"; see "The Religion of the Inner Light," printed in the current volume. In 1930, Rufus Jones and the English Quaker Henry Hodgkin (1877–1933), a co-founder of the Fellowship of Reconciliation, established Pendle Hill in Wallingford, Pennsylvania, as a retreat center.

I can't name him so it's all right—met several times to see if there could be founded a center in the Philadelphia area to which people could come to spend a week on occasion for retreats, to spend a year during which courses in religion, meditation, ethics as applied to the human condition and a sense of family would be developed. There would be no servants, everybody shared everything. You helped with the cooking until you are not permitted to do it anymore, and the dishes, cutting the wood: everything was done by those people sharing it. And silences were obtained, and very rigid academic demands were made on the mind but no degrees. And people come from all over the country to spend a summer there, or a winter. And it is an interesting commitment of form of the Quaker ethos to both the intellectual and the social conditions of mankind. There are courses or seasons of retreats; people come from famine areas and spend a month, two months, three months sharing what they have seen and felt. Some of the greatest things happen when you are washing the dishes and taking your turn cooking. Now this is Rufus at his best. The combination of the mind and the day-by-day ordinary experiences of ordinary life dedicated to the relief of human suffering. These two things moved always in everything that he wrote, every lecture that I ever heard him give, every sermon he has ever preached, as nearly as I can ascertain it. He was working at the integration of the God of the mind, the God notion, the God idea, and the God of experience. When he was thinking creatively and poetically about the God of the mind, then at once he was sure that this God lighted every person that came into the world. This was the inner light, a part of the givenness of God. When he was thinking in the other dimension, he could not separate his sense of religious experience and Christian piety from one of the demands that would come into the life of an individual only after he'd been visited by the spirit of Jesus Christ. So that you see this ambivalence moving all the time. And I'm very grateful that he did not ever resolve it; for my own reasons I am very grateful.

Now one other sentence about him. The test of his mysticism, for him, was the way that it enabled him to transcend the maladies of his organism. A very simple thing but terribly important. He had, for instance, he had an incipient hay fever that became so asthmatic that life wasn't worth living, and he and the timeless juices of the eternal made some sort of potion and he got it out of the way. He had a terrible accident in which various bones, ribs, and all kinds of things were smashed up, and he felt that if his experience of God is as he claims it to be in his life, then this ought to provide the resource by which he could even transcend the pain and not be berserked by it.[44] So as soon as they trussed him up or whatever they do to people, they brought him to Haverford in an ambulance, set him up in his room with his feet up on these weights, and with something else somewhere else. And the first day after he arrived his classes started meeting. They would come in his sick room and sit on the floor, and he went on lecturing until he could walk. He felt that the life of God that is in us is never on holiday—never on holiday. And it is always concerned about fulfilling itself in everything it touches. And the contribution that he made to my thought, and then we'll stop.

First, he helped me define and give a name to experiences that were a part of my life ever since I can remember. Second, he introduced me to the concept of mysticism, which concept was completely foreign to my whole frame of reference. But when I got it, I had a handle now and a handle that is very important. [Another] contribution that he made to me was to help me block out the territory that for the rest of my life I would be exploring. And this to me was very, very important, the most fundamental contribution that could have been made to my life at that time. I was in my late twenties, and I wanted to get a road map because I had a very high-powered car, and I wanted to be sure I could see far enough ahead so as not to wreck either myself or anybody who got in my way. And Rufus helped me. And so, I blocked out areas of exploration and reading and thinking in which I have been working all of my life. And I am very grateful to him because it enabled me to put a fence, it doesn't matter how far out that way or this way the fence was, the fact that I had a sense of a fence that there was a boundary. And where there is no boundary there is no meaning. This he helped me do. So, I tolerated my feelings and forgave me of my negative feelings because I didn't ever feel that he could ever get off the dime and deal, make the Quakers practice religion with Negroes. I just—I forgave him. We'd talk about it now and then, not often because as soon as we'd start talking about it he would take wings, you know, and it was just wonderful, I just enjoyed his flight, but I was still trying to mess

---

44. Jones had a serious automobile accident in 1923.

around with this thing, you know. But it helped me understand. It did not even cross his mind when I asked for this radical and unusual thing, that a question of my color had anything to do with it at all. I thought he was being wise and sort of putting me quietly in my place because I had raised the question. So, when he answered he said nothing about it; he just didn't, and then there wasn't anything. I bird-dogged his mind, and there wasn't a thing that gave me any feeling that he was not transcending whatever the bind was that I was in. Now I don't know how to put this any other way, but I've been trying to figure it out forty years, but, and I think it's because the first thing that came through to me from him was, here was a man to whom the angels had spoken and into whose ears God has whispered, and I could trust his words.

One other thing—all right, I'll stop in a minute. What would you do without somebody riding herd on you? He's carrying out his orders.

The thing that I marvel at in Rufus was the fact that in his presence you felt that you were in the presence of a great spirit, but in his presence, you felt that you were a great spirit, you see. As contrasted, for instance, with Tagore. When we spent three-and-a-half hours in the presence of [Rabindranath] Tagore in Santiniketan, and you know he sat in this chair and you were afraid to breathe lest you disturb something. And every now and then he would focus on your presence and say something, and you'd hold your breath, and then he'd take off again, and you'd wait until he came back.[45] But you didn't want to uncross your legs. You know it was like going to be interviewed for a job, and you stand at the desk, and here is this somebody sitting there who has power of life and death over your days, and he scrutinizes you and you wonder whether the third button on your shirt is buttoned or not, but you dare not look. I mean it's that kind of thing. But Rufus had all of this enormous sense of presence and yet so completely a part of whatever your limitations, your ignorances. From him always came a ladder, and you could climb it to see the vision which

---

45. Thurman met the Bengali poet and author Rabindranath Tagore (1861–1941), the first non-Western winner of the Nobel Prize for Literature (1913), in his school in Santiniketan, near Calcutta, in January 1936, as a part of the tour of the Negro Delegation to India. As Thurman indicated, though he admired Tagore's magnificent beard, he found him to be too oracular, and the conversation left him somewhat disappointed (WHAH 128–29, 135).

he saw as the figure, you remember in Tennyson's "In Memoriam"—man wanders and he looks trying to find a way to heaven, and in his exhaustion he falls and he discovers that where he falls he is at the foot of a ladder that goes straight to heaven.[46] Now this is the quality of this man; I will always love him because he opened a way in my thinking and will always be identified with that way. I have no interest in whether my thoughts and his thoughts clash or are one; all that is irrelevant. But he opened up a way for my heart as the only other great teacher that I had opened up the way for my mind.

---

46. Alfred Lord Tennyson, "In Memoriam A.H.H.," (1850), stanza 55, ll. 12–16: "I falter where I firmly trod/And falling with the weight of cares/Upon the great world's altar-stairs/That slope thro' darkness up to God."

Selected Bibliography

Printed Primary Sources

Thurman, Howard Washington. *For the Inward Journey: The Writings of Howard Thurman.* Edited by Anne Spencer Thurman and Vincent Harding. New York: Harcourt Brace Jovanovich, 1984.

———. *Howard Thurman: Essential Writings.* Edited by Luther E. Smith. Maryknoll, NY: Orbis Books, 2006.

———. *The Papers of Howard Washington Thurman.* Edited by Walter Earl Fluker. Volumes 1–5. Columbia: University of South Carolina Press, 2009–19.

———. *Sermons on the Parables.* Edited by David B. Gowler and Kipton Jensen. Maryknoll, NY: Orbis Books, 2018.

———. *A Strange Freedom: The Best of Howard Thurman on Religious Experience and Public Life.* Edited by Walter Earl Fluker and Catherine Tumber. Boston: Beacon, 1998.

———. *Moral Struggle and the Prophets.* Volume 1 of *Walking with God: The Sermon Series of Howard Thurman.* Edited by Peter Eisenstadt and Walter Earl Fluker. Maryknoll, NY: Orbis Books, 2020.

Books by Howard Thurman

Thurman, Howard Washington. *The Greatest of These.* Mills College, CA: Eucalyptus, 1944.

———. *Jesus and the Disinherited.* New York: Abingdon-Cokesbury, 1949.

———. *Deep Is the Hunger: Meditations for the Apostles of Sensitiveness.* New York: Harper & Brothers, 1951.

———. *Meditations of the Heart.* New York: Harper & Brothers, 1953.

———. *The Creative Encounter: An Interpretation of Religion and the Social Witness.* New York: Harper & Brothers, 1954.

———. *Deep River and the Negro Spiritual Speaks of Life and Death*. New York: Harper & Brothers, 1955.

———. *The Growing Edge*. New York: Harper & Brothers, 1956.

———. *Footprints of a Dream: The Story of the Church for the Fellowship of All Peoples*. New York: Harper & Brothers, 1959.

———. *Mysticism and the Experience of Love*. Wallingford, PA: Pendle Hill, 1961.

———. *Disciplines of the Spirit*. New York: Harper & Row, 1962.

———. *The Luminous Darkness: A Personal Interpretation of the Anatomy of Segregation and the Ground of Hope*. New York: Harper & Row, 1964.

———. *The Centering Moment*. New York: Harper & Row, 1969.

———. *The Search for Common Ground: An Inquiry into the Basis of Man's Experience of Community*. New York: Harper & Row, 1971.

———. *A Track to the Water's Edge: The Olive Schreiner Reader*. New York: Harper & Row, 1973.

———. *The Mood of Christmas and Other Celebrations*. New York: Harper & Row, 1973.

———. *The First Footprint: The Dawn of the Idea of the Church for the Fellowship of All Peoples*. San Francisco: Lawton & Alfred Kennedy, 1975.

———. *With Head and Heart: The Autobiography of Howard Thurman*. New York: Harcourt Brace Jovanovich, 1979.

Secondary Sources on Howard Thurman

Bennett, Lerone, Jr. "Howard Thurman: 20th Century Holy Man." *Ebony* 33, no. 4 (February 1978): 68–70, 72, 76, 84–85.

Burden, Jean. "Howard Thurman." *Atlantic Monthly*, October 1953, 39–44.

Dixie, Quinton, and Peter Eisenstadt. *Visions of a Better World: Howard Thurman's Pilgrimage to India and the Origins of African American Nonviolence*. Boston: Beacon, 2011.

Eisenstadt, Peter. *Against the Hounds of Hell: A Life of Howard Thurman*. Charlottesville: University of Virginia, 2021.

Ellison, Gregory C., II, ed. *Anchored in the Spirit: Discovering Howard Thurman as Educator, Activist, Guide, and Prophet.* Louisville, KY: Westminster John Knox, 2020.

Fluker, Walter E. *They Looked for a City: A Comparative Analysis of the Ideal of Community in the Thought of Howard Thurman and Martin Luther King, Jr.* Lanham, MD: University Press of America, 1989.

Gandy, Samuel Lucius, ed. *Common Ground: Essays in Honor of Howard Thurman on the Occasion of His Seventy-Fifth Birthday, November 18, 1975.* Washington, DC: Hoffman, 1976.

Harding, Vincent. Foreword to Howard Thurman, *Jesus and the Disinherited.* Boston: Beacon, 1996.

Harvey, Paul. *Howard Thurman and the Disinherited.* Grand Rapids, MI: Eerdmans, 2020.

Jackson, Kai Issa, and Arthur L. Dawson. *Howard Thurman's Great Hope.* New York: Lee & Low, 2008.

Jensen, Kipton E. *Howard Thurman: Philosophy, Civil Rights, and the Search for Common Ground.* Columbia: University of South Carolina Press, 2019.

Makechnie, George K. *Howard Thurman: His Enduring Dream.* Boston: Howard Thurman Center, Boston University, 1988.

Millet, Ricardo A., and Conley H. Hughes, eds. *Debate and Understanding: Simmering on the Calm Presence and Profound Wisdom of Howard Thurman.* Special issue, 1982.

Mitchell, Mozella G., ed. *The Human Search: Howard Thurman and the Quest for Freedom—Proceedings of the Second Annual Thurman Convocation.* New York: Peter Lang, 1992.

———. *Spiritual Dynamics of Howard Thurman's Theology.* Bristol, IN: Wyndham Hall, 1985.

Neal, Anthony Sean. *Howard Thurman's Philosophical Mysticism: Love against Fragmentation.* Lanham, MD: Lexington, 2019.

Pollard, Alton. *Mysticism and Social Change: The Social Witness of Howard Thurman.* New York: Peter Lang, 1992.

Siracusa, Anthony C. *The World as It Should Be: Religion and Nonviolence before King.* Chapel Hill: University of North Carolina, 2021.

Smith, Luther E. *Howard Thurman: The Mystic as Prophet*. Lanham, MD: University Press of America, 1981.

Yates, Elizabeth. *Howard Thurman: Portrait of a Practical Dreamer*. New York: John Day, 1964.

Young, Henry James. *God and Human Freedom: A Festschrift in Honor of Howard Thurman*. Richmond, IN: Friends United Press, 1983.

Index of Names

Abraham (biblical patriarch), 24, 125
Adams, Henry, 28, 29n9
Adams, Marian ("Clover") Hooper, 29n9
Adeodatus (son of Augustine), 49n17
Adler, Alfred, 30n12
Aitken, Guy, 155n40
Allen, James Lane, 27n6
Ambrose, Nancy, xvi
Ambrose, Saint, 47, 47n15, 48, 49, 49n17
Anaximenes, 52n20
Anderson, Victor, 92n6
Appelbaum, Patricia, 62n1
Aristotle, 52, 128, 128n6
Arnold, Matthew, 148, 148n22
Augustine of Hippo, Saint, xixn24, 1n1, 24n14, 34, 39, 39n6, 43–53, 55, 148

Baader, Franz von, 82n2, 91n3
Bacon, Francis, 105, 105n3
Barr, Roberta Byrd, xvin15
Basil of Caesarea, Saint, 47n15
Bennett, Lerone, Jr., xxi, xxin34
Bergoglio, Jorge Mario, 68n11
Beuningen, Coenraad van, 98n15
Blake, James, 11n5
Blake, William, 1n1, 2, 3n4, 10–18, 80, 80n23, 100n18

Blanshard, Paul, 84n8
Boehme, Jacob, 1n1, 2, 3n4, 11, 11n4, 13, 91–102, 137
Boucher, Catherine, 12n7
Bowling, Richard H., xiiin2
Bridges, Hal, xivn6
Brinton, Anna, 95n9
Brinton, Howard Haines, 94, 94–95n9, 95
Bro, Marguerite Harmon, xixn26
Brown, Peter, 46n12
Buddha, xviii, 2n2, 3n4, 25–33, 55, 56
Bunyan, John, 135n14
Burden, Jean, xvn10

Cary, Henry Francis, 110n10
Catherine of Siena, Saint, 75n11
Cayce, Edgar, xix, xixn26
Cheney, Sheldon, 3, 3–4n4
Churchill, Winston, 153n38
Clark, Glenn, 153, 153n36, 154
Columbus, Christopher, 106
Constantine, Emperor, 50n18
Cook, Enid Appo, 152n34

Damon, S. Foster, 13n8
Damrosch, Leopold, 13n8
Dana, Peter, xivn3
Dante Alighieri, 104, 109, 109n9, 110n10

166 INDEX OF NAMES

Darwin, Charles, 65, 66n6
Debs, Eugene, 17, 17n14
Desai, Mahadev, 54n2
Deutero-Isaiah (Second Isaiah), 79, 80
Dixie, Quinton, 54n2
Dunn, Rev. J. E., xix, xixn26

Eckhart, Meister (Eckhart, Johannes), xx, 1n1, 2, 3n4, 5n5, 52, 52n21, 67, 82–90, 115n3, 119, 136, 136n16, 137, 141, 142, 145
Eckhart von Hochheim. *See* Eckhart, Meister
Edwards, M. J., 37n4
Eisenstadt, Peter, 24n11, 29n10, 54n2, 126n5, 132n11, 139n19, 141n2, 143n8
Eliade, Mircea, xvn12
Ellis, Havelock, 48, 48n16
Elman, Mischa, 66, 67n7
Emerson, Ralph Waldo, 39, 39–40n9, 61, 61n8
Ewer, Mary Anita, xiv, xviiin7, 83, 83n4

Filoramo, Giovanni, 91n3
Fischer, Kevin, 100n18
Fluker, Walter Earl, xxiin38, 93n7, 101n19
Fox, George, 113, 113n2, 117, 149n26, 156, 156n43
Fra Angelico, 2, 3n4
Francis, Pope. *See* Bergoglio, Jorge Mario
Francis of Assisi, Saint, 1n1, 62–71, 74, 146, 147n20
Franck, Sebastian, 91n2

Galsworthy, John, 28, 28n8

Gandhi, Mohandas Karamchand "Mahatma," xiv, xxi, 1, 1n1, 26, 26n3, 32, 32n15, 54–61, 149n26
Goethe, Johann Wolfgang von, 91n3
Gordian III, 36n2
Gowler, David B, 39n7
Granger, Lester, xiv, xv, xvn8
Grosskurth, Phyllis, 48n16
Guyon, Madame Jeanne, 146, 146n18, 146n19

Hamilton, Alexander, 144, 144n11
Hardy, Clarence E., III, xvin12
Harrison, Ted, 69n12
Hedstrom, Matthew S., 149n25
Hegel, Georg Wilhelm Friedrich, 82n2, 91n3, 147, 147n21
Hermerken, Thomas. *See* Thomas à Kempis
Heydrich, Reinhard, 154–55n40
Hicks, Elias, 149n23
Hinkleman, Benjamin, 98n13
Hitler, Adolf, 154
Hodgkin, Henry, 156n43
Holmes, Edmond Gore Alexander, 84n7
Houdini, Harry, xiv
Huizinga, Johan, 106n4

Innocent III, Pope, 68n11
Isaac (biblical patriarch), 24, 125

Jacob (biblical patriarch), 24, 125
James, William, 75n11, 142n6
Jaspers, Karl, 21n5
Jenness, Mary, xvi, xvin14
Jensen, Kipton, 39n7
Jesus, 8, 14n9, 16, 17, 20, 21, 24, 26, 31, 38, 39n6, 39n7, 68, 69, 75,

Index of Names

113n2, 116, 121, 125, 128, 138, 155, 155n42, 156, 157
Joan of Arc, 106, 106n5
John of the Cross, Saint, 135, 135n13, 146n17
John XXII, Pope, 85n10
Jones, E. Stanley, 153, 153n37, 154
Jones, Lucius L., Jr., xiiin2
Jones, Rufus, xvii, xviin18, xviii, xix, xx, xxi, 1, 1n1, 2, 54, 62n2, 82, 92n5, 95, 99n16, 141–60

Kabir, 75n11, 136, 136n15
Katz, Steven V., 19n2
Kelley, Katie, 69n13
Kenney, John Peter, 46n12
Kepler, Johannes, 40, 40n10

Lao-Tse, 3n4, 19–24
Legge, James, 27n6
Leuba, James H., 146, 146n19
Lincoln, Abraham, 65, 66n6
Louder, Virgil, xv

Malin, Patrick, 152n33
Mays, Benjamin E., xvi, xvin14
McCall, Oswald, 123n2, 129n8
McCombs, William, 6, 7, 7n7
McGinn, Bernard, 86n13
Mendelssohn, Felix, 65, 66n6
Milton, John, 14n9
Mitchell, Mozella Gordon, 122n1
Monica, Saint, 47n14, 49
Montague, Margaret Prescott. *See* Steger, Jane
Mukerji, Dhan Gopal, 130n10
Myers, J. Arthur, 69n13

Napoleon, 65

Neal, Anthony Sean, xivn5
Niebuhr, Reinhold, xxii
Noyes, Alfred, 78, 78n19

O'Regan, Cyril, 82n2
Oetinger, Friedrich, 91n3
Origen, 47n15

Pagels, Elaine, 129n7
Paine, Thomas, 15n12
Panhke, Walter N., xix, xixn26
Patricius (father of Augustine of Hippo), 47n13
Paul (biblical author), 21, 39n6, 43n2, 89
Pelagius, 45, 45n7
Peter (apostle), 138
Phelps, Dryden, 20n3, 95, 95n10
Phillips, Dorothy, 83n4
Philo, 47n15
Pietro di Bernardone (father of St. Francis), 67n8
Pilate, Pontius, 155n42
Pio, Padre, 69n12
Pitt, William, the Younger, 15n12
Plato, 24n12, 36n2, 37, 51, 52, 53, 128n6, 128n7
Plotinus, 1, 1n1, 2, 3n4, 34–42, 47n15, 53, 87, 137
Porphyry, 37n4

Raboteau, Albert J., xxiin37
Rhodes, Harrie Vernette, xix, xixn26
Richter, Gregorius, 98n12, 98n15, 99n16
Rodin, Auguste, 129, 129n8
Ronkey, Mr. and Mrs., 77, 77n18
Roosevelt, Franklin D., 153, 153n38
Roosevelt, Theodore, 6n6

Index of Names

Rosenberg, Ethel, 73n8
Rosenberg, Julius, 73n8
Royce, Josiah, 142n6

Saint-Gaudens, Augustus, 28, 29n9
Sandberg, Carl, 66, 66n7
Schreiner, Olive, xvi, xvii, xxi, 73, 73n6, 132, 132n11, 149, 149n24
Schwenkfeld von Ossig, Caspar, 91n2
Scott, Robert, 18n16
Shakespeare, William, 105, 105n3
Shaw, George Bernard, 155n42
Siddhartha Gautama. *See* Buddha
Smith, J. Y., xivn4
Smith, Luther E., xivn5, 122n1, 141n2
Socrates, 37
Stannard, Mary Newton, 72n4
Steere, Douglas V., xx, xxn29, 145, 145n14
Steger, Jane, 1, 72–81
Stiles, William C., 18n16
Stoudt, John Joseph, 91n1
Suso, Heinrich, 75n11, 82

Taft, William Howard, 6n6
Tagore, Rabindranath, 75n11, 159, 159n45
Tardieu, Michel, 44n6
Tauler, Johannes, 82
Tennyson, Alfred Lord, 8n8, 20n4, 28, 39n9, 160, 160n46

Teresa of Avila, Saint, 146n17
Thomas à Kempis, 103–11
Thompson, Francis, 39, 39n8
Thurman, Saul Solomon, 99n17
Tietjens, Eunice, 155n41
Tolstoy, Leo, 73n8, 81, 81n27, 118
Traherne, Thomas, 75n11
Tynan, Kathleen, 63n3, 64n4

Underhill, Evelyn, xviii, xviiin22, 75, 75n11

Valentinus, 91n3, 128n7
Vining, Elizabeth, 141, 141n1, 143n6, 149n26
Virgil, 104, 109, 110n10

Waterman, Nixon, 17n15, 132n12
Watson, Finely M. K., 72n4
Watson, John B., 30, 30n13
Watt, Homer A., 72n4
Weigel, Valentine, 91n2
Whittier, John Greenleaf, 143n10, 147
Wilson, Woodrow, 6, 6n6, 7n7
Woolman, John, 149n26
Wordsworth, William, 39n9

Young, Henry J., 122n1